Intermediate Reader of Modern Chinese

Vocabulary   Sentence Patterns   Exercises

Intermediate Reader of Modern Chinese

Vocabulary   Sentence Patterns   Exercises

Chih-p'ing Chou   Der-lin Chao

周質平   趙德麟

Princeton University Press

1992

Library of Congress Cataloging-in-Publication Data

Chou, Chih-p'ing, 1947-
      Intermediate reader of modern Chinese / Chih-p'ing Chou, Der-lin
  Chao.
        p.   cm.
      Chinese and English.
      Includes index.
      Contents: [1] Text -- [2] Vocabulary, sentence patterns,
  exercises.
      ISBN 0-691-01529-5 (PB)
      1. Chinese language--Textbooks for foreign speakers--English.
  2. Chinese language--Readers.   I. Chao, Der-lin, 1957- II. Title.
  PL1129.E5C438   1992

  495.1'86421--dc20   92-2679

The publisher would like to acknowledge the authors of this volume for

providing the camera-ready copy from which this book was printed

Printed in the United States of America

10

ISBN-13: 978-0-691-01529-3 (pbk.)

ISBN-10: 0-691-01529-5 (pbk.)

目錄

Intermediate Reader of Modern Chinese

Vocabulary   Sentence Patterns   Exercises

第一課

給爸爸媽媽的信

Vocabulary

開學	开学	kāixué kaishyue	VO:	"open school", opening of school, school starts
學期	学期	xuéqī shyuechi	N:	semester
選課	选课	xuǎn-kè sheuan-keh	VO:	"choose courses", to select courses, to take courses
門	门	mén men	M:	measure word for courses
物理		wùlǐ wuhlii	N:	physics
化學	化学	huàxué huahshyue	N:	chemistry
經濟	经济	jīngjì jingjih	N:	economics; economy
歷史	历史	lìshǐ lihshyy	N:	history
決定	决定	juédìng jyuedinq	N:	decision
專業	专业	zhuānyè juanyeh	N:	(academic) major, specialty, expertise
不同		bùtóng butorng	Adj: N:	different difference
或許	或许	huòxǔ huohsheu	Adv:	perhaps, maybe, probably
發現	发现	fāxiàn fashiann	V:	to discover, to find out
興趣	兴趣	xìngqù shinq.chiuh	N:	interest

1

從小　从小	cóngxiǎo tsorngsheau	Adv:	from childhood
科學　科学	kēxué keshyue	N:	science
進　　进	jìn jinn	V:	to enter
大學　大学	dàxué dahshyue	N:	college
文學　文学	wénxué wenshyue	N:	literature
相當　相当	xiāngdāng shiangdang	Adv:	quite, rather
重	zhòng jonq	Adj:	heavy (in weight); difficult and overloaded (in courses, work, etc.)
尤其	yóuqí youchyi	Adv:	especially
教授	jiàoshòu jiawshow	N:	professor
嚴　　严	yán yan	Adj:	strict (of persons), rigorous (of rules and regulations)
實驗　实验	shíyàn shyryann	V: N:	to experiment experiments, labs (in a science course)
經常　经常	jīngcháng jingcharng	Adv:	often, frequently
報告　报告	bàogào bawgaw	V: N:	to report report; paper
時間　时间	shíjiān shyrjian	N:	time (span)
雙人房　双人房	shuāngrénfáng shuangrenfarng	N:	double room
同屋ㄦ	tóngwūr torng'ul	N:	roommate
年級　年级	-niánjí -nianjyi	M/N:	grade, year (of school or course of study)

半夜	bànyè bannyeh	TW:	in the middle of the night (after 12:00 A.M.)
這一點　这一点	zhèi-yì-diǎn jey-i-dean		this point (in the abstract sense)
光是	guāngshì guang.sh	Adv:	solely, just
花錢　花钱	huā-qián hua chyan	VO:	to spend money
回信	huí-xìn hwei-shinn	VO: N:	"return letter", to reply (to a letter) a reply (to a letter)
寄	jì jih	V:	to mail
支票	zhīpiào jypiaw	N:	a check (money)
敬祝	jìngzhù jinqjuh	V:	to respectfully offer (good wishes from someone of lower status to someone of higher status) (NOTE: This is a common salutation for letters and is not spoken.)
健康	jiànkāng jiannkang	Adj: N:	healthy health 敬祝健康: (a conventional closing for a letter)
女兒　女儿	nǚ'ér neu'erl	N:	daughter (NOTE: In signing a letter the writer uses a title to explain his relationship to the recipient, e.g., 兒,學生,友,母)
小芬	Xiǎofēn Sheaufen		name of daughter (NOTE: In the closing of a letter one usually uses only his first name, not his last name.)
敬上	jìngshàng jinqshanq		respectfully offer (this letter (from lower to higher)) (Convention used after the signature in a letter)

Sentence Patterns

1.　A 對 B 有 興 趣　　　A is interested in B

⊙　我進了大學以後才知道自己對文學，歷史也很有興趣。
I didn't find out that I was also interested in literature and history until after I entered college.

(1)　我對歷史很有興趣。
I'm very interested in history.

(2)　張先生對看電影有沒有興趣？
Is Mr. Chang interested in watching movies?

(3)　他對文學沒有興趣。
He is not interested in literature.

(4)　我對這本書完全沒有興趣。
I have no interest in this book whatsoever.

2.　尤 其　　　especially, particularly

⊙　這幾門課都相當重，尤其是化學課。
These several courses are quite difficult, especially chemistry.

尤 其 SV

(1)　他們家的人都很高，他父親尤其高。
The people in his family are all very tall; his father is especially tall.

(2)　這兒的東西都很貴，吃的東西尤其貴。
Everything here is expensive; food is especially expensive.

尤 其 V

(3)　我不喜歡吃中國菜，我尤其不喜歡吃南方菜。
I don't like to eat Chinese food, I especially don't like to eat Southern (Chinese) food.

(4)　我喜歡看電影，我尤其喜歡看美國電影。
I like to watch movies; I especially like to watch American movies.

尤 其 N

    (5)   我喜歡吃中國菜，尤其是南方菜。
          I like to eat Chinese food, especially Southern food.

    (6)   我討厭做家事，尤其是洗碗。
          I hate doing housework, especially washing dishes.

3.   **Question Words + 都**   indicating inclusiveness

⊙   她甚麼都好，就是男朋友的電話太多。
    Everything about her is good, it's just that her boyfriend calls too much.

    (1)   你在哪儿住都行。
          Wherever you live is alright.

    (2)   多麼貴的書我都買得起。
          No matter how expensive the books are, I can afford them.

    (3)   我怎麼做他都不高興。
          However I do it, he's not happy.

    (4)   張先生誰都喜歡。
          Everyone likes Mr. Chang. (or) Mr. Chang likes everyone.
          Note: The 誰 in this sentence can be either the subject or the object
          of the verb 喜歡.

    (5)   你甚麼時候來都可以。
          Whatever time you come is fine.

4.   **Question Words + 都 ...就 是**   The 就 是 phrase indicates
                                exclusiveness

⊙   她甚麼都好，就是男朋友的電話太多。
    Everything about her is good, it's just that her boyfriend calls too much.

    (1)   你在哪儿住都行，就是別住在學校宿舍。
          Wherever you live is alright, just don't live in the school's
          dormitory.

    (2)   誰都要去就是他不想去。

Everyone wants to go, only he doesn't want to go.

(3) 我甚麼時候都有空，就是星期三沒有空。
I'm free any (other) time, it's just Wednesday that I'm busy.

(4) 這本書甚麼都好，就是太貴。
Everything about this book is good, it's just too expensive.

5. 還沒 ... 呢   still have not ...

⊙ 有幾本書還沒買呢！
There are several books (I) still haven't bought!

(1) A: 你的書買了沒有？
A: Have you bought your books (yet)?

B: 我有好幾本書還沒買呢。
B: There are quite a few books I haven't bought yet.

(2) A: 你早飯吃了沒有？
A: Have you eaten breakfast?

B: 我還沒吃呢。
B: I still haven't eaten.

(3) A: 你妹妹畢業了吧？
A: I suppose your little sister has graduated?

B: 她還沒畢業呢。
B: She still hasn't graduated.

還在 V 呢   still V-ing

(1) 已經上午十一點了，他還在睡覺呢。
It's already eleven (o'clock), and he's still sleeping.

(2) 大家都吃完了，只有他一個人還在吃呢。
Everyone's done eating, only he is still eating.

(3) 他還在看書呢，真用功。
He's still studying. (He's) really diligent.

6. 光是 A 就 B   only, merely, just

⊙ 光是物理課的書就花了一百五十多塊錢。
Just for the books for my physics class, I spent over one hundred and fifty dollars.

(1) 光是預備中文課就花了三個鐘頭。
(He) spent three hours just preparing for the Chinese lesson.

(2) 在美國上大學很貴。光是住宿舍就要兩千塊錢。
Attending college in America is very expensive. It costs two thousand dollars alone to live in the dormitory.

(3) 整理屋子真麻煩，光是掃地我就覺得累得不得了。
Cleaning house is really a pain. Just sweeping the floor tires me out.

Excercises

一．完成對話　(Complete the following dialogues using the expressions in parentheses.)

1. A: 在這個大學念書貴不貴？

   B: 貴得要命，＿＿＿＿＿＿＿＿＿＿＿＿＿＿＿＿＿＿。

   （光是 ... 就 ...）

2. A: 這學期你的課怎麼樣？

   B: ＿＿＿＿＿＿＿＿＿＿＿＿＿＿＿＿＿＿＿＿＿。

   （甚麼都 ... 就是 ...）

3. A: 你昨天買的書貴不貴？

   B: ＿＿＿＿＿＿＿＿＿＿＿＿＿＿＿＿＿＿＿＿＿。

   （尤其 V）

4. A: 你的同屋怎麼樣？

   B: ＿＿＿＿＿＿＿＿＿＿＿＿＿＿＿＿＿＿＿＿＿。

   （甚麼都 ... 就是 ...）

5. A: 這個學校的老師都很有名嗎？

   B: ＿＿＿＿＿＿＿＿＿＿＿＿＿＿＿＿＿＿＿＿＿。

   （尤其 N）

二．翻譯　(Translation)

1. I am very interested in history. However, since I am already taking four courses, I don't know whether I'll be able to take it .

2. I dislike the laboratory course, especially the professor, because he often makes us write papers.

3. Although the professor is very strict with students, and often gives us exams, he teaches very well. That's why everyone takes his course.

4. I spent more than three hundred dollars on my Chinese textbooks. Now, I don't have even one dollar.

5. Do people who are interested in literature like to read books on history?

6. This semester all my courses are very tough. Just doing an experiment requires five hours per week. Therefore, I am going to do nothing but study.

三．作文　　(Composition)

Write a letter to your parents telling them about (i) your school life, (ii) your courses, and (iii) your needs.

第二課

爸爸的回信

Vocabulary

來信 来信	láixìn laishinn	V: N:	"come letter", to receive a letter (incoming) letter
收到	shōudào shoudaw	RV:	to receive (a letter, check, etc.) (NOTE: the object must be concrete)
沒想到	méi xiǎngdào mei sheangdaw	RV:	(I) did not expect that ...
記得 记得	jìde jih.de	V:	remember
小學 小学	xiǎoxué sheaushyue	N:	elementary school, primary school
討厭 讨厌	tǎoyàn taoyann	V: Adj:	to strongly dislike annoying, vexing, disgusting
居然	jūrán jiuran	Adv:	actually (contrary to expectation); to (my) surprise; unexpectedly
讓　让	ràng ranq	V:	to make
爲了 为了	wèile wey.le		in order to; for the sake of
畢業 毕业	bìyè bihyeh	V:	to graduate
找	zhǎo jao	V:	to look for
一些	yì-xiē i-shie	Adj:	some, several, a few
並（不／沒） 并（不／沒）	bìng (bù/méi) binq (bu/mei)	Adv:	(intensifier used with a negative) (not) in fact, (not) really

結果 结果	jiéguǒ jyeguoo	Adv: N:	as a result result
不一定	bùyídìng bu idinq	Adv:	not necessarily
好處 好处	hǎochù haochuh	N:	advantage, good or strong points **壞處**: negative points
剛 刚	gāng gang	Adv:	just (a short time before)
需要	xūyào shiuyaw	V: N:	to need a need
筆 笔	bǐ bii	M:	for a large sum of money, e.g. 一 **大筆錢**
緊 紧	jǐn jiin	Adj:	tight, short of money, time, etc.
沒法	méifǎ meifaa		there is no way, (here) it's very difficult
臨時 临时	línshí linshyr	Adj:	temporary
賺錢 赚钱	zhuàn-qián juann-chyan	VO:	to earn money
零用錢 零用钱	língyòngqián lingyonqchyan	N:	"odds-and-ends use money", pocket money
月底	yuèdǐ yuehdii	TW:	at the end of the month
發 发	fā fa	V:	to distribute (or to receive as a result of distribution) **發薪水**: to distribute or to receive as salary
薪水	xīnshǔi shinshoei	N:	salary
到時 到时	dàoshí daw shyr		when the time comes (written)
最近	zuìjìn tzueyjinn	TW:	recently

11

圖書館 图书馆	túshūguǎn twushugoan	N:	library
週末 周末	zhōumò joumoh	TW:	weekend
上班	shàng-bān shanq-ban	VO:	to go to work, to be at work
吵架	chǎo-jià chao-jiah	VO:	to argue, to quarrel
祝	zhù juh	V:	to wish
學業 学业	xuéyè shyueyeh	N:	schoolwork (formal usage - not spoken) (colloquial: 功課，作業)
進步 进步	jìnbù jinnbuh	V: Adj: N:	to improve, to make progress advanced, improved improvement, progress 學業進步: a common wish for students
爸	bà bah		father (NOTE: Because the letter is written by the father to his child, 敬上 is not used.)

Sentence Patterns

1.　居然　　　surprisingly, unexpectedly

⊙　你在小學的時候常說最討厭歷史課，現在居然也喜歡文學、歷史了。
When you were in elementary school, you always said that you hated history. Now you surprisingly like literature and history.

(1)　我們已經二十多年沒見了，他居然還記得我的名字。
It's already been twenty years since we have seen each other, (but) surprisingly he still remembers my name.

(2)　他在日本住了好幾年，沒想到居然一句日本話都不會說。
He lived in Japan for a number of years. It did not occur to me that he (surprisingly) would not be able to speak even one sentence of Japanese.

2.　讓　　　to make; to cause

⊙　這讓我很高興。
This makes me very happy.

(1)　這件事讓我很高興。
This matter makes me very happy.

(2)　弟弟不喜歡上學讓父母很生氣。
My little brother's dislike of school makes my parents very angry.

3. 為了   in order to

⊙ 很多人為了畢業以後找工作，學一些自己並不喜歡的課。
In order to find a job after graduation, many people take courses that they themselves don't like.

(1) 為了學好中文，他跟中國人住在一塊儿。
In order to learn Chinese well, he lives with Chinese people.

(2) 為了找一個好工作，他去念大學。
In order to find a good job, he went to college.

...是為了

(3) 他跟中國人住在一塊儿是為了學好中文。
He lived with Chinese people in order to learn Chinese.

(4) 他去念大學是為了找一個好工作。
He went to college in order to find a good job.

為了 + noun phrase   for the sake of N; because of N

(5) 為了生活，他一天到晚努力工作。
For the sake of living, he works hard day and night.

(6) 為了工作，我可以不睡覺。
For the sake of work, I don't have to sleep.

4. A對 B有好處   A is beneficial to B

⊙ 多選一些不同的課,對你是很有好處的。
Taking more different courses is beneficial to you.

(1) 運動對身體有好處。
Exercise is beneficial to your health.

(2) 喝酒對你沒有好處。
Drinking is not good for you.

(3) 會說中文對找工作有沒有好處？
Is knowing Chinese beneficial in finding a job?

5. **連...都/也...** even (intensive stressing the comparative degree)

⊙ 有時連週末都得上班。
Sometimes I even have to work on weekends.

連 + noun

(1) 媽媽連週末都得上班。
Mom even has to work on weekends.

(2) 他做的飯連狗都不吃。
Even dogs won't eat his cooking.

(3) 他連我說的話都不相信。
He won't even believe what I say.

(4) 他連明天的功課都做好了。
He even finished tomorrow's homework.

連 + verb construction

(1) 這麼小的屋子，連我一個人住都太小。
This room is so small, even if I live alone, it's still too small.

(2) 他連我穿甚麼顏色的衣服都管。
He even wants to control what color clothes I wear.

(3) 他看報的時候連別人跟他說話都聽不見。
When he reads the paper, he can't even hear other people speaking to him.

Excercises

一．完成對話　(Complete the following dialogues with the expressions in parentheses.)

1.　A: 你為什麼做臨時工作？

　　B: ＿＿＿＿＿＿＿＿＿＿＿＿＿＿＿＿＿＿＿＿＿＿。
　　　　　　　　　　　　　　　　　　　　　　　　　（為了．．．）

2.　A: 你那麼不喜歡科學，為什麼選這門課呢？

　　B: ＿＿＿＿＿＿＿＿＿＿＿＿＿＿＿＿＿＿＿＿＿＿。
　　　　　　　　　　　　　　　　　　　　　　　（．．．是為了．．．）

3.　他是美國人可是他 ＿＿＿＿＿＿＿＿＿＿＿＿＿＿＿＿。
　　　　　　　　　　　　　　　　　　　　　　　　　（居然）

4.　A: 你為什麼學中文？

　　B: ＿＿＿＿＿＿＿＿＿＿＿＿＿＿＿＿＿＿＿＿＿＿。
　　　　　　　　　　　　　　　　　　　　　　　（對．．．有好處）

5.　A: 王先生會不會說中文？

　　B: ＿＿＿＿＿＿＿＿＿＿＿＿＿＿＿＿＿＿＿＿＿＿。
　　　　　　　　　　　　　　　　　　　　　　　（連．．．都．．．）

6.　A: 你能不能明天早上九點鐘到學校來？

　　B: ＿＿＿＿＿＿＿＿＿＿＿＿＿＿＿＿＿＿＿＿＿＿。
　　　　　　　　　　　　　　　　　　　　　　　　　（才）

二．　翻譯　(Translation)

1.　Money has been very tight recently. I won't be able to send you the check until next week.

2.　When taking a course, the most important thing is to have a strict professor. It doesn't matter if the workload is heavy or not.

3. A: It's already the end of the month, and I still haven't been paid. I don't even have money to buy food.

   B: Since you don't have any money, let's eat at home this weekend.

4. In order to carry out experiments, I don't even have time to look for a part-time job this semester. My spending (pocket) money is extremely tight now.

5. The students working in the library are all very annoying, especially the one who likes to quarrel with others.

三． 作文 (Composition)

請你說一說你的專業（會）是什麼？你怎麼決定你的專業？

第三課

電話

Vocabulary

喂	wéi (wèi) wei (wey)	Intj:	hello (as a telephone greeting)
李小芬	Lǐ Xiǎofēn Lii Sheaufen		a name
請…聽電話 请…听电话	qǐng...tīng- diànhuà chiing...ting- diannhuah		"please have ... come listen to the phone" I would like to speak to ... (NOTE: 請 ... 接電話 can also be used)
剛剛 刚刚	gānggāng gangx		just now
大概	dàgài dahgay	Adv:	probably
上	shàng shanq		to go (a place)
廁所 厕所	cèsuǒ tsehsuoo	N:	bathroom
都…了	dōu ... le dou ... le		It's already ...
快	kuài kuay	Adv:	almost, soon
來電話 来电话	lái diànhuà lai diannhuah	VO:	to give (me) a call (cf. 來信)
擔心 担心	dān-xīn dan-shin	VO: Adj:	to worry to be worried
餐廳 餐厅	cāntīng tsanting	N:	dining hall; restaurant
乾淨 干净	gānjìng ganjinq	Adj:	clean

肚子	dùzi duhtz	N:	stomach, belly
把肚子吃壞了 把肚子吃坏了	bǎ dù.zi chī-huài.le baa duhtz chy-huay .le		to have upset one's stomach by eating something
跑	pǎo pao	V:	(frequently) to hurry to, to rush to
瀉　　泻	xiè shieh	V:	to have diarrhea
大夫	dàifū day.fu	N:	a doctor (more colloquial than 醫生)
醫院　医院	yī'yuàn i'yuann	N:	hospital
拉肚子	lā-dùzi lha-duhtz	VO:	"pull stomach", to have the "runs", to have diarrhea
發燒　发烧	fā-shāo fa-shau	VO:	to have a fever
瘦	shòu show	V: Adj:	to lose weight, to become thin thin
好幾　好几	hǎo-jǐ hao-jii	Det:	"a goodly several", quite a few
磅	bàng banq	N:	a pound
老	lǎo lao	Adv:	always
減肥　减肥	jiǎn-féi jean-feir	VO:	"cut fat", to lose weight, to diet
吃不下	chību-xià chy.bu-shiah	RV:	"eat-not-down", can't eat, don't feel like eating, can't finish eating
水果	shuǐguǒ shoeiguoo	N:	fruit
噢，對了 噢，对了	O, duìle Oh, duey.le	Intj:	Oh, yes (remembering something else)

期中考	qīzhōngkǎo chijongkao	N:	mid-term examination
要命	yàomìng yawminq		"demand-life; to a life-threatening point," extremely, ... to death 忙得要命: extremely busy, busy to death
找藉口　找借口	zhǎo-jièkǒu jao-jiehkoou	VO:	to look for excuses
藉口　借口	jièkǒu jiehkoou	N:	an excuse
實在　实在	shízài shyrtzay	Adv:	truly, really
最多	zuì duō tzuey duo	Adv:	at most
篇	piān pian	M:	measure word for articles, termpapers
頁　页	yè yeh	M/N:	page 第一頁: first page 三頁: three pages
題目	tímù tyimuh	N:	topic, title
急死我了	jí-sǐ wǒ le jyi-syy woo.le		I'm worried to death
怪	guài guay	V:	to blame
關心　关心	guānxīn guanshin	V: Adj: N:	to be concerned about concerned concern
洗碗	xǐ-wǎn shii-woan	VO:	"wash-bowl", to wash dishes
碗	wǎn woan	N: M:	一個碗: a bowl 一碗飯: a bowl of rice)
小時　小时	xiǎoshí sheaushyr	N:	an hour (same as 鐘頭)

低	dī di	Adj:	low
工資 工资	gōngzī gongtzy	N:	wages
功課 功课	gōngkè gongkeh	N:	schoolwork, homework
忙不過來 忙不过来	mángbú-guòlái mang.bu-guohlai	RV:	"unable to handle the business", too busy, to have too much to do
幹嘛 干嘛	gànmá gannma		"why on earth?" (colloquial)
像 象	xiàng shianq	V:	to resemble, to seem, as (similar)
願意 愿意	yuànyì yuann.yih	Aux:	to be willing to
反對 反对	fǎnduì faanduey	V:	to oppose

Sentence Patterns

1. （都）快 ...了

⊙ 到現在都快十天了，你也沒來個電話。
Up until now it has been almost ten days, and you still haven't called.

(1) 都快考試了，他還沒開始念書。
It will soon be exam time, and he has still not started studying.

(2) 都快吃晚飯了他才回來。
He didn't return until it was almost time to eat supper.

(3) 他去了都已經一個月了，只打過一次電話。
He's been gone for a month already and has called only once.

(4) 都快十二點了，你怎麼還不睡？
It's almost twelve o'clock. Why are you still up?

2. A 跟 B 有關係   A is related to B; A has something to do with B

⊙ 這幾天很多人拉肚子，大概跟餐廳的飯有關係。
These past several days many people have had diarrhea. It's probably related to the cafeteria food.

(1) 拉肚子跟餐廳的飯有關係。
Diarrhea is related to the cafeteria food.

(2) 我不想上大學跟錢沒有關係。
My not wanting to go to college has nothing to do with money.

(3) 他這次生病跟天氣有沒有關係？
Does the weather have anything to do with his getting sick this time?

3. （倒）是 ... 可是（就是）... actually/really
... the only thing is ...

⊙ 燒倒是沒有，就是不想吃東西。
It's really not a fever, I just don't want to eat anything.

(1) 日本車貴倒是不貴就是太小。
Actually Japanese cars aren't expensive, it's just that they are too small.

(2) 這本書難倒是不難，就是字太小，看不清楚。
This book is really not that hard, it's just that the words are too small and unclear.

(3) 這所學校有名倒是有名，就是離我家遠了一點。
This school is famous alright, it's just that it is a little too far from home.

4. Frequency

In Chinese, the way to indicate frequency is to combine a time expression (span of time) with a measure word for verbs. The word order is just the opposite of the English.

⊙ 每星期十小時
Ten hours a week

Used without a verb

(1) 一個月一次
once a month

(2) 一個星期兩次
twice a week

(3) 半個鐘頭一次
once every half hour

(4) 半年一次
once every half-year / semi-annually

Used with a verb-object

    (5)   一個月看一次電影
              watch a movie once a month

    (6)   一個星期吃兩次館子
              eat out twice a week

    (7)   半個鐘頭上一次廁所
              go to the bathroom twice every hour

    (8)   半年回一次家
              return home once every half year

Topic-Comment

    (9)   (電影)一個月看一次
              watch a movie once a week

    (10)   (館子)一個星期吃兩次
              eat out twice a week

    (11)   (廁所)半個鐘頭上一次
              go to the bathroom once every half hour

    (12)   (家)半年回一次
              return home once every half year

5.   A 以後再 B   do B after A; wait until A then B

⊙   期中考以後再開始。
    I'll start after the mid-term exams are over.

    (1)   我現在不想工作，期中考以後再開始工作。
              I don't want to work right now. I'll start working after the mid-term exams.

    (2)   我現在不想念書，吃過晚飯以後再念書。
              I don't want to study right now. I'll study after I have finished eating dinner.

6. **既然** given the fact that; since it is the case that; now that

⊙ 既然你自己願意做工賺點儿錢，我也不反對。
Since you are willing to work and earn some money, I won't object.

既然 A 就 B (吧)

(1) A: 我餓了。
    A: I'm hungry.

    B: 既然你餓了，就去吃飯吧。
    B: Since you're hungry, then eat.

(2) A: 坐火車真慢。
    A: Taking the train is slow.

    B: 既然你覺得坐火車慢，就坐飛機吧。
    B: Since you feel taking the train is slow, then take the plane.

(3) A: 對不起，我明天不能來。
    A: Sorry, I can't come tomorrow.

    B: 既然你明天不能來就後天來吧。
    B: Since you can't come tomorrow, then come the day after tomorrow.

(4) 既然人口很多，人民的生活水平當然不高。
    Since the population is so large, the people's standard of living is certainly not high.

既然 + rhetorical question

(1) A: 我餓了。
    A: I'm hungry.

    B: 既然你餓了，你為甚麼還不去吃飯呢？
    B: Since you're hungry, why haven't you eaten yet?

(2) A: 坐火車真慢。
    A: Taking the train is really slow.

    B: 既然坐火車很慢，你怎麼不坐飛機呢？
    B: Since taking the train is so slow, how is it you don't take the plane?

Excercises

一．完成對話　　(Complete the following dialogues with the expressions in parentheses.)

1. A: 我想跟他到紐約 (New York)去，可是明天我們有考試。

   B: _____。

   （既然 with a suggestion）

2. A: 我選了這位教授的課，可是聽說他的課相當重。

   B: _____？

   （既然 with a rhetorical question）

3. A: 你為什麼不買那本書？是不是太貴了？

   B: _____。

   （倒是 ...，就是 ...）

4. A: 我要去看電影，你跟我一塊儿去，好不好？

   B: _____。

   （...以後再 ...）

5. A: 他不上大學是因為沒有錢嗎？

   B: _____。

   （A跟B(沒)／有關係）

二．　　翻譯　　(Translation)

1. I got a letter from my father. In addition, he sent me a check for five hundred dollars. I have to call him tonight to thank him.

2. People who want to lose weight need to exercise more. Besides that, they need to eat less rice and more fruit.

3. A: My stomach doesn't feel well.
   B: If that is the case then why don't you go see a doctor?

4. What he hates most is to wash dishes. Every time his mother asks him to wash dishes he says that he has to study. He is really good at finding excuses.

5.   A: You are going to graduate in June. Now it's almost April, why haven't you started to look for a job?

      B: Didn't you tell me before that to earn lots of money is not important?

      A: Don't look for excuses. I am concerned about you. Your parents just called. They asked me to tell you that they will not send a check to you this month.

6.   In order to lose weight I only eat once a day. As a result, I have lost 3 pounds.

三.   作文   (Composition)

1.   Please write a telephone conversation.

2.   Write a letter to your teacher explaining why you didn't go to class on a certain day.

第四課

申請工作

Vocabulary

申請 申请	shēnqǐng shenchiing	V:	to apply for
先生	xiānshēng shian.sheng	N:	mister (title)
約 约	yuē iue	V:	to set an appointment or date
面談 面谈	miàntán mianntarn	V: N:	"face-talk", to have an interview interview
見 见	jiàn jiann	V:	to see or to meet someone (for a special or offical purpose)
長途 长途	chángtú charngtwu	Adj:	long-distance
辦公室 办公室	bàngōngshì banngongshyh	N:	office
旅行社	lǚxíngshè leushyngsheh	N:	travel agency, tour operator
介紹 介绍	jièshào jieh.shaw	V:	to introduce
東亞研究	DōngYà yánjiū DongYah yanjiou	N:	East Asian Studies
東亞 东亚	DōngYà DongYah		East Asia
研究	yánjiū yanjiou	V: N:	to research research, studies
夏天	xiàtiān shiah.tian	N:	summer 冬天: winter 春天: spring 秋天: fall

28

趟	tàng tanq	M:	number of times (going, coming, etc.)
除了…以外	chúle ... yǐwài chwu.le ... yiiway		besides, in addition to...
學習 学习	xuéxí shyueshyi	V: N:	to study, to emulate study, studies
參加 参加	cānjiā tsanjia	V:	to join (a group), to participate in
旅遊團 旅游团	lǚyóutuán leuyoutwan	N:	tour group
上海	Shànghǎi Shanqhae	PW:	Shanghai
蘇州 苏州	Sūzhōu Sujou	PW:	Soochow, Suzhou
南京	Nánjīng Nanjing	PW:	Nanking, Nanjing
北京	Běijīng Beeijing	PW:	Beijing (Peking)
經驗 经验	jīngyàn jingyann	V: N:	to experience experience
幫助 帮助	bāngzhù bangjuh	V: N:	to help help
起先	qǐxiān chiishian	Adv:	at first
帶 带	dài day	V:	(here) to guide, to lead (a tour)
學歷 学历	xuélì shyuelih	N:	educational background (formal usage)
經歷 经历	jīnglì jinglih	N: V:	(here) professional experience (formal) to experience
銀行 银行	yínháng yinharng	N:	"silver store", bank

待遇		dàiyù dayyuh	N:	compensation, salary, treatment
差		chà chah	Adj:	inferior, lacking
高中		gāozhōng gaujong	N:	senior high school
翻譯	翻译	fānyì fanyih	V: N:	to translate, to interpret translation; translator; interpreter
筆譯	笔译	bǐyì biiyih	N:	(written) translation
口譯	口译	kǒuyì koouyih	N:	oral translation, interpretation
日常		rìcháng ryhcharng	Adj:	daily
會話	会话	huìhuà hueyhuah	N:	conversation
應付	应付	yìngfù yinq.fuh	V:	to handle, to deal with, to cope with
填		tián tyan	V:	to fill in (a form)
表		biǎo beau	N:	a form
交		jiāo jiau	V:	(here) to hand in, to submit
秘書	秘书	mìshū mihshu	N:	secretary
在…之內		zài ... zhīnèi tzay ... jyney		within (a certain range of time, space, etc.)
通知		tōngzhī tongjy	V: N:	to inform, to notify notification; a notice
姓名		xìngmíng shinqming	N:	full name (formal)
性別		xìngbié shinqbye	N:	sex (male, female) (formal)

地址	dìzhǐ dihjyy	N:	address
出生年月日	chūshēng nián yuè rì chusheng nian yueh ryh	N:	year, month, and date of birth (formal)
公	gōng gong	N:	short for 辦公室
市立	shìlì shyhlih	Adj:	"city-established", established and administered by the city", municipal
職員　职员	zhíyuán jyryuan	N:	staff member
私立	sīlì sylih	Adj:	privately administered, private
教員　教员	jiàoyuán jiawyuan	N:	"teaching staff", faculty (formal)
婚姻	hūnyīn huen'in	N:	marriage
狀況　状况	zhuàngkuàng juanqkuanq	N:	situation, condition
未婚	wèihūn weyhuen	Adj:	"not yet married", single (formal)
已婚	yǐhūn yiihuen	Adj:	"already married", married (formal)
離婚　离婚	líhūn lihuen	V:	to divorce
導游　导游	dǎoyóu daoyou	N:	tour guide
目前	mùqián muhchyan	TW:	at present
職位　职位	zhíwèi jyrwèi	N:	professional position, status, rank
及	jí jyi	Conj:	and (written)

年薪	niánxīn nianshin	N:	annual salary
美金	měijīn meeijin	N:	U.S. dollars
元	yuán yuan	M/N:	dollar (formal)
備註 备注	bèizhù beyjuh	N:	"prepare for (further) note/comment" comments (on a form)

Sentence Patterns

1. 約   to set up an appointment or date with someone

⊙ 昨天我跟他在電話裡約好了，今天三點來跟他面談。
Yesterday I made an appointment with him by phone to come see him at three o'clock today.

   (1)   我約他明天去看電影。
I made a date with him to see a movie tomorrow.

   (2)   他約我去打球。
He made a date with me to play ball.

   (3)   我跟他約好了，明天兩點在圖書館見面。
I made an appointment with him. We will meet tomorrow at two o'clock in the library.

   (4)   我跟牙醫約好了，今天下午去看牙。
I made an appointment with the dentist for this afternoon to have a check-up.

   (5)   這幾天我很忙，要是你想來看我得先跟我約好。
These past few days I've been very busy. If you want to see me you must first make an appointment with me.

2. 一 ... 就 ...   whenever; as soon as; once .... then ....

⊙ 電話一打完就請您進去。
As soon as he has finished calling, please go in.

Used with one subject

   (1)   我一吃涼的東西（我）就不舒服。
As soon as I eat cold things, I don't feel well.

   (2)   我一看書（我）就想睡覺。
As soon as I start reading, I want to sleep.

   (3)   （我）一想到這件事我就生氣。
As soon as I think about this I get angry.

(4)　　（我）一打電話我就緊張。
As soon as I call I get nervous.

Used with two different subjects

(5)　　老師一生氣學生就不敢說話了。
As soon as the teacher gets angry, the students don't dare speak up.

(6)　　你一說我就懂了。
As soon as you said it I understood.

(7)　　我們一上車，他就唱起歌來了。
As soon as we got into the car, he started singing.

3.　是 [來 / 去] V 的　　expresses purpose in coming or going

⊙　我是來申請工作的。
I have come to apply for a job.

(1)　　我不是來找王先生的，我是來找王太太的。
I have not come to look for Mr. Wang, I'm here to look for Mrs. Wang.

(2)　　你是不是到這儿來念書的？
Did you come here to study?

(3)　　我下個月去紐約，是去開會的不是去買東西的。
Next month I'm going to New York to attend a meeting, not to go shopping.

4.　除了...以外，還 / 也...

⊙　除了學習中文以外，還參加了一個旅遊團。
Aside from studying Chinese, I have also participated in a tour group.

(1)　　我除了會說中文以外還會說日文。
Besides being able to speak Chinese, I can also speak Japanese.

(2)　　這個學期除了物理以外我也選了化學跟歷史課。

This semester, besides physics, I am also taking chemistry and history.

(3) 除了王先生以外，李先生也對文學有興趣。
Besides Mr. Wang, Mr. Li is also interested in literature.

5. A, B, C, . . . 這 些（這 Num M）N

Gives a series of examples of the topic in question. Word order is the opposite of English.

⊙ 我到過上海、蘇州、南京、北京這些地方。
I have been to these places: Shanghai, Soochow, Nanking and Peking.

(1) 他的皮包裡有筆、錢、眼鏡這些東西。
Her purse has such things as pens, money and glasses in it.

(2) 像跑步、打球這些運動對身體都有好處。
Exercises like running and playing ball are beneficial to your health.

6. A 對 B 有 幫 助   A is helpful to B

⊙ 不知道這些經驗對你們的工作有沒有幫助。
I don't know if these experiences will be beneficial to your work.

(1) 多吃水果對身體有幫助。
Eating more fruit is good for your health.

(2) 這本書對你寫報告有沒有幫助？
Is this book useful to you in writing your paper?

(3) 你的意見好是好，可是對這件事沒有甚麼幫助。
Your opinion is good alright, but it's not much help in this matter.

7.　在 ... 之內　　　　　within ...

⊙　我們會在一星期之內把結果通知你的。
We will notify you of the results within a week.

(1)　在一個星期之內我得把報告寫完。
I must finish writing my paper within a week.

(2)　他在一個月之內能不能把那本書翻譯完？
Can he finish translating that book within one month?

(3)　在三哩之內你找不到別的中國飯館。
You couldn't find another Chinese restaurant within three miles.

Excercises

一．完成對話　(Complete the following dialogues with the expressions in parentheses.)

1. 老師：今天是星期一，請你們在下個星期一以前把報告寫完。

　　學生：老師要我們 _____。
　　　　　　　　　　　　　　　　　　　　　（在⋯之內）

2. A: 今年夏天你到中國去旅行的時候去了哪些地方？

　　B: _____。

3. A: 你給小丁打電話了嗎？

　　B: 我打了，_____。
　　　　　　　　　　　　　　　　　　　　　（約）

4. A: 你為什麼到這儿來？

　　B: _____。
　　　　　　　　　　　　　　　　　　　　　（是⋯的）

二．　翻譯　(Translation)

1. I don't know whether these work experiences are helpful in applying for this job.

2. Besides 小張, Mr. 王 is also joining that tour group.

3. The teacher asked us to finish the translation exercises in three days.

4. My major was economics. After graduation, I worked in a bank for a year. Later, since the pay was bad, I quit the job.

5. Next summer, I will join a tour group to travel in China because I don't speak Chinese well. Even though I can handle the everyday speech, I will sometimes need the tour guide to translate.

6. Your professional experience and your educational background will be very helpful in this job.

7. His major is East Asian Studies. He is especially interested in China. In order to study Chinese history, he has been to China twice. While he was in China, in addition to doing research, he also taught in a college.

三．　作文　(Composition)

1. You are applying for a job as a Chinese teacher in an American high school.

   (i) Draw a 工作申請表 then fill it in with your personal information. (ii)Write a one page interview conversation.

2. You have just heard of a job related to your major and have made an appointment with the manager to discuss your qualifications. Please write a dialogue between yourself and the manager.

第五課

信 （一）

Vocabulary

强姦	强奸	qiángjiān chyangjian	V: to rape N: rape
偷竊	偷窃	tōuqiè touchieh	N: theft (formal)
結束	结束	jiéshù jyeshuh	V: to end, to finish N: the end
計劃	计划	jìhuà jihhuah	V: to plan N: a plan
暑假		shǔjià shuujiah	N: summer vacation
忙着		mángzhe mangj	to be busy with
暑期		shǔqī shuuchi	N: summertime (formal)
準備	准备	zhǔnbèi joenbey	V: to prepare; to plan to N: preparation
語言	语言	yǔyán yeuyan	N: language
外語	外语	wàiyǔ wayyeu	N: a foreign language
份		fèn fenn	M: measure word for jobs and other things (that imply an allotment) 一份報: newspapers 一份工作: a job
短期		duǎn-qī doan-chi	Adj: short-term
經理	经理	jīnglǐ jinglii	N: manager

用	yòng yonq	V:	to employ, to use
想不到	xiǎngbúdào sheang.bu-daw	RV:	"wasn't able to think of", unexpected
站	zhàn jann	V:	to stand
櫃台　柜台	guìtái gueytair	N:	counter
顧客　顾客	gùkè guhkeh	N:	customer
提錢　提钱	tíqián tyi-chyan	VO:	to withdraw money
存錢　存钱	cún-qián tswen-chyan	VO:	to deposit money, to save money
電子計算機 电子计算机	diànzǐ-jìsuànjī dianntzyy- jihsuannji	N:	"electronic calculating machine", computer 電腦: "electric brain", computer
到…爲止 到…为止	dào … wéizhǐ daw … weijyy		up to (a certain time, place, or extent)
成績　成绩	chéngjī cherng.ji	N:	grades, achievement
成功	chénggōng chernggong	V: Adj: N:	to succeed successful success
其他	qítā chyita	Adj:	other
發生　发生	fāshēng fasheng	V:	to occur, happen
害怕	hàipà haypah	V:	to be scared
照相機　照相机	zhàoxiàngjī jawshianqji	N:	camera
被	bèi bey		a passive marker (see note)

偷	tōu tou	V:	to steal
校園　校园	xiàoyuán shiawyuan	PW:	campus
同系	tóngxì torngshih		(to be) in the same department
系	xì xi	N:	department
班	bān ban	N:	class
開會　开会	kāi-huì kai-huey	VO:	to attend or have a meeting
晚會　晚会	wǎnhuey woanhuey	N:	evening party 開晚會：to hold a party 開會：to hold a meeting
酒	jiǔ jeou	N:	liquor, wine
一直	yìzhí ijyr	Adv:	continuously, all through
開車　开车	kāi-chē kai-che	VO:	to drive (a car)
湖	hú hwu	N:	lake
邊　　边	biān bian	N:	side
聊天	liáo-tiān liau-tian	VO:	"talk weather", to chat
據說　据说	jùshuō jiuhshuo		it is said that ...
自願　自愿	zìyuàn tzyhyuann		willing, voluntary
同情	tóngqíng torngchyng	V: N:	to sympathize with sympathy

堅持 坚持	jiānchí jianchyr	V:	to insist on, persist in
被迫	bèipò beypoh	Adj:	to be coerced, to be forced
還　还	hái hair	Adv:	still, yet, even
上報 上报	shàng-bào shanq-baw	VO:	to appear in the newspapers
警察	jǐngchá jiingchar	N:	police
報社 报社	bàoshè bawsheh	N:	newspaper office
記者 记者	jìzhě jihjee	N:	reporter
生活	shēnghuó shenghwo	N:	life
影響 影响	yǐngxiǎng yiingsheang	V: N:	to influence, to affect impact
簡直	jiǎnzhí jeanjyr	Adv:	simply, as in 'simply too ...'
聽說 听说	tīngshuō tingshuo	V:	to hear (it said)
強暴	qiángbào chyangbaw	V:	rape; to rape
案件	ànjiàn annjiann	N:	(criminal) case
女生	nǚshēng neusheng	N:	female student, young woman
報案 报案	bào-àn baw-ann	VO:	to report (a case) to the police
可怕	kěpà keepah	Adj:	scary, frightening

Sentence Patterns

1.   忙著   to be busy (doing something)

⊙   有些人忙著找暑期工作。
Some people are busy looking for summer jobs.

(1)   快要期中考了，大家都忙著預備功課。
It will soon be mid-terms. Everyone is busy preparing for the exam.

(2)   A: 你這幾天在忙(些)甚麼？
A: What have you been busy doing for the past few days?

B: 我忙著整理屋子。
B: I'm busy straigtening up my room.

(3)   我每天忙著做功課。
I am busy every day doing homework.

2.   到 ... 為止   up to (a certain time or degree)

⊙   到現在為止，我的成績都很好。
Up to now, my grades have been very good.

(1)   到明天為止，我在這兒已經住了兩年了。
By tomorrow, I will have already lived here for three years.

(2)   我們今天上課就到下午三點為止。
We will have class until three o'clock today.

(3)   到現在為止，他還沒回來。
Up to now, he still has not returned.

(4)   跑步就跑到那條街為止。
Jog up to that street.

(5)   你們可以吃到飽為止。
You can eat until you are full.

(6)   聽錄音帶得聽到能記住為止。
Listen to the tape until you have it memorized.

43

3. 除了 ... 以外　　except for

⊙　除了化學課有幾個實驗做得不成功以外，其他幾門課大概都是A。
I probably got an A in all of my classes except for chemistry, in which I had a few unsuccessful experiments.

(1)　除了小張以外，別的人都是這個大學畢業的。
Except for Little Zhang, all the others graduated from this university.

(2)　除了這本書，桌子上只有一枝筆。
Besides this book, only one pen is on the table.

(3)　除了我以外沒有人會說中文。
Besides me, no one else can speak Chinese. (Only I can speak Chinese.)

4. 被　　Passive voice marker

⊙　有一個男同學的照相機被偷了。
A male student's camera was stolen.

(1)　A: 魚被貓（給）吃了。
A: The fish was eaten by the cat.

B: 魚被吃了。
B: The fish was eaten.

(2)　A: 糖都被狗吃完了。
A: All the candy was eaten by the dog.

B: 糖被吃完了。
B: The candies were eaten.

(3)　你的書被他（給）拿走了。
Your book was taken away by him.

(4)　杯子被弟弟打破了。
The cup was broken by (his) younger brother.

44

5. 一直 V 到 . . . . . （為 止）

Indicates that an action continues up to a certain point.

⊙ 晚會一直開到早上三點。
The party lasted until three o'clock in the morning.

(1) 他開會一直開到十二點。
His meeting lasted until twelve o'clock.

(2) 他每天念書一直念到把每一個生字都記住了為止。
Every day he studies until he has memorized every vocabulary item.

6. A 對 B 有 影 響   A has an impact on B; A influences B

⊙ 這件事對我的生活有很大的影響。
This event has had a great impact on my life.

(1) 汽車對人的生活有很大的影響。
Cars have a great influence on people's lives.

= 汽車影響人的生活。
Cars influence people's lives.

= 人的生活受汽車的影響。
People's lives are influenced by cars.

(2) 中文對日文有很大的影響。
The Chinese language has had a great influence on the Japanese language.

= 中文影響了日文。
The Chinese language has influenced the Japanese language.

= 日文受到了中文的影響。
The Japanese language has been influenced by the Chinese language.

Excercises

一．完成對話
(Complete the following dialogues with the expressions in parentheses.)

1.　A: 你的好朋友常常給你寫信嗎？

　　B: ＿＿＿＿＿＿＿＿＿＿＿＿＿＿＿＿＿＿＿＿＿＿。

　　　　　　　　　　　　　　　　　　　（到 . . .為止）

2.　A: 為甚麼他從來不洗衣服？

　　B: ＿＿＿＿＿＿＿＿＿＿＿＿＿＿＿＿＿＿＿＿＿＿。

　　　　　　　　　　　　　　　　　　　（忙著）

3.　A: 美國的經濟跟日本的經濟有沒有關係？

　　B: ＿＿＿＿＿＿＿＿＿＿＿＿＿＿＿＿＿＿＿＿＿＿。

　　　　　　　　　　　　　　　　　　　（影響）

4.　A: 昨天的晚會是什麼時候結束的？

　　B: ＿＿＿＿＿＿＿＿＿＿＿＿＿＿＿＿＿＿＿＿＿＿。

　　　　　　　　　　　　　　　　（一直 V 到 . . .（為止））

5.　A: 這個學期你選了五門課，這五門課的成績都很好嗎？

　　B: ＿＿＿＿＿＿＿＿＿＿＿＿＿＿＿＿＿＿＿＿＿＿。

　　　　　　　　　　　　　　　　　　　（除了）

二．改寫句子
(Rewrite the following sentences with the expressions provided. Maintain the original meaning.)

1.　在我選的課裡只有中文課的成績是 A。

　　= ＿＿＿＿＿＿＿＿＿＿＿＿＿＿＿＿＿＿＿＿＿＿。

　　　　　　　　　　　　　　　　　　　（除了）

2.　他把我賺的錢都花完了。

　　= ＿＿＿＿＿＿＿＿＿＿＿＿＿＿＿＿＿＿＿＿＿＿。

　　　　　　　　　　　　　　　　　　　（被）

三． 翻譯　　(Translation)

1. According to the newspaper, the college campus is dangerous. Except for the camera that was stolen, which belonged to the male student who often calls my roommate, no other bad things have happened. Actually, living on campus is not dangerous at all.

2. I am sympathetic toward people who work in a bank. They have to stand behind a counter all day long helping customers deposit or withdraw money.

3. Last week, I attended a party. Everyone drank a lot of wine. The party finished at midnight. After I returned to my dormitory, I chatted with my roommate until eight o'clock in the morning.

4. Somebody stole my roommate's camera and computer last week, but up to now nobody knows who did it.

5. There have been many cases of rape on campus. However not many women were willing to report (it) to the police. Sometimes when the women did report (it) to the police, the man (involved) would insist that the woman had been willing.

6. Because I haven't graduated from college, I can't be a manager in the bank. My job is just to help the customers deposit or withdraw money.

7. My summer plans for this year are to go to a language school and learn a foreign language. I don't think that I will have time to have a short-term job.

四． 作文　　(Composition)

1. Write a letter to your parents telling them about (i) a recent crime that happened on campus, (Please see the announcement below) and give your reflections on this matter. (ii) comments on your courses (Don't forget your Chinese class!) and your study plans for the upcoming semester.

> At approximately 10:00 PM, Monday, January 2, 1989 a female student was assaulted by an unknown male assailant while she was studying alone in a public area of Wilson College. The victim was both struck with a fist and received a puncture wound in her back. After striking the victim the assailant fled.
>
> The victim described her assailant as a black male, 18-22 years old, 5'4" - 5'8" tall, dark complexion, wearing gray ski jacket, gray or tan pants, a gray knit hat, and wearing gloves.
>
> You should exercise extra caution when moving about campus. Walk with a friend, call Public Safety - 3134 for an escort, or ride the Public Safety Shuttle. Always lock you dormitory room door and windows. Do not study alone in lounges or study areas.

Proctors and Princeton Borough Police are investigating. If you have any information concerning this crime call one of these agencies as soon as possible.

Alert issued 1/2/89   11:00 p.m.

(2) Explain why the following two characters have become well-known in the area of Middlebury. What advice would you give to other students? Be creative: <u>do not</u> simply translate the words of the "Advisory". <u>Ten</u> sentences at least.

SAFETY ADVISORY
MIDDLEBURY COLLEGE SECURITY   POSTED: 7/8/88

ATTENTION: The two composites are of individual's involved in two Sexual Assault/ Harassment cases in the Middlebury area.

- #1 Is a composite of a male subject involved in a reported suspicious activity around Lake Dunmore.

- #2 Is a composite from an incident which occurred in Cornwall on 6/27/88.

NOTE: Both composites have similar characteristics. Both suspects mid-twenties with blondish hair, med. build.

SUSPECT VEHICLES: #1. 1984/85 green sedan in good condition, hatchback with sticker across entire rear window, bucket seats with wooly type covers.

#2. Vehicle was small well kept, silver blue/similar to Honda hatchback.

IF YOU HAVE ANY INFORMATION ON TEH ABOVE INDICENTS, OR IF YOU MAY KNOW OR HAVE SEEN THESE INDIVIDUALS, PLEASE CONTACT THE DEPARTMENT OF SECURITY AT EXT. 5911 OR THE MIDDLEBURY POLICE AT 388-3191. YOUR COOPERATION IS APPRECIATED.

第六課

信 （二）

Vocabulary

同居	tóngjū torngjiu	V:	to live together
危險　危险	wēixiǎn ueishean	Adj: N:	dangerous danger
像　　像	xiàng shianq	Adv:	like, as (similar)
可能	kěnéng keeneng	Adv: N: Adj:	probably, possibly possibility possible
平常	píngcháng pyngcharng	TW: Adj:	usually, ordinarily ordinary, common
深夜	shēnyè shenyeh	TW:	"deep night", late at night
附近	fùjìn fuhjinn	PW:	vicinity
工廠　工厂	gōngchǎng gongchaang	N:	factory
如果	rúguǒ ruguoo	Conj:	if, supposing that
自從⋯以後 自从⋯以后	zìcóng ... yǐhòu tzyhtsorng ... yiihow		ever since ...
希望	xīwàng shiwanq	V: N:	to hope hope
段	duàn duann	M:	measure word for segment (of time, paragraph, space, etc.)

交朋友	jiāo-péngyǒu jiau-perng.yeou	VO:	make friends
整天	zhěngtiān jeengtian	TW:	all day long, the whole day
混	hùn huenn	V:	"to mix", to keep company with, to run around with (derogatory)
不是···就是···	búshì A jiùshì B bu.sh A jiow.sh B		if it's not A, then it's B; it must be either A or B
跳舞	tiàowǔ tiawwuu	VO:	"jump dance", to dance
許多　许多	xǔduō sheuduo	Adj:	many
帶　　带	dài day	V:	to take, to lead (someone)
不以爲然 不以为然	bù yǐ wéi rán bu yii wei ran		"(I) don't think that's the case", to object
才	cái tsair		only, just
高三	gāosān gausan		senior (3rd year) in high school
技能	jìnéng jihneng	N:	skills
維持　维持	wéichí weichyr	V:	to maintain, to preserve
生活	shēnghuó shenghwo	N: V:	(daily) life to live
緊張　紧张	jǐnzhāng jiinjang	Adj:	tense
觀念　观念	guānniàn guan'niann	N:	concept
落伍	luòwǔ luohwuu	Adj:	"fall behind the line", out of date, behind the times

只要···就···	zhǐyào ... jiù jyyyaw ... jiow		as long as ...
相愛　相爱	xiāng'ài shiang'ay	V:	to love each other
一起	yìqǐ ichii		together
結婚　结婚	jiéhūn jyehuen	V:	to get married
意見　意见	yìjiàn yihjiann	N:	opinion

Sentence Patterns

1. 又...又...　　　both ... and... ; not only ... but also...

⊙　校園裡太危險了，又有偷竊又有強姦。
The campus is too dangerous, There are robberies as well as rapes.

(1)　學校裡又有讀書的地方，又有運動的地方。
There are both study and exercising areas in the school.

(2)　我又餓又累，得休息休息吃點兒東西才行。
I am both hungry and tired. I must rest and eat something.

(3)　這個學校，老師又好，學生又聰明，所以很有名。
At this school the teachers are good and the students smart.
Therefore it is very famous.

(4)　小狗又跑又跳，高興得不得了。
The puppy is both running and jumping. He is extremely happy.

(5)　他又會唱歌，又會跳舞。
He can both sing and dance.

2. 自從...以後...　　　ever since ...

⊙　自從你上了大學以後，一年最多在家一個月。
Ever since you went to college, you are home for only one month per year
at most.

(1)　自從1979年以後，我一直住在美國。
From 1979 on, I have continuously lived in the USA.

(2)　我自從學了中文以後，認識的中國人越來越多了。
Ever since I learned Chinese, I have met more and more Chinese
(people)

3. 不是 ... 就是 ...　　　if (it's) not ..., then (it's) ...

⊙ 兩個人整天混在一起，不是喝酒，就是跳舞。
The two of them hang around all day together. If they are not drinking, then they are dancing.

(1) 世界上只有兩種人，不是男的就是女的。
There are only two kinds of people in this world. If you are not male, then you're female.

(2) 我每天不是念書就是工作，生活真沒有意思。
Everyday, if I'm not studying, then I'm working. Life is simply not interesting.

4. 只要 ... 就 ...　　　as long as ... then ...

⊙ 男女只要相愛就可以生活在一起。
As long as a man and woman love each other, then they can live together.

(1) 這本書只要你喜歡我就給你。
As long as you like this book I'll give it to you.

(2) 只要你肯請我吃飯我就幫你的忙。
As long as you are willing to treat me to a meal, I'll help you.

(3) 在美國，只要有錢就可以買你喜歡的東西。
In America, as long as you have money, you can buy anything you like.

只要 ... A not A 又有甚麼關係呢？
As long as ... what does it matter whether or not A?

(1) 房子只要住得舒服，漂亮不漂亮又有甚麼關係呢？
As long as the house is comfortable, what does it matter whether it's beautiful or not?

(2) 朋友只要性情好，有錢沒有錢又有甚麼關係呢？
As long as a friend's personality is good, what does it matter whether he has money or not?

5. 才　　only; just

⊙　他現在才高三，就想跟女朋友同居。
He's only in his third year of high school and already wants to live with his girlfriend.

(1)　這本書才三塊錢，真便宜！
This book is only three dollars. How cheap!

(2)　他今年才十五歲，怎麼能上大學呢？
This year he is only 15. How can he attend college?

6. 用...來...　　use ... to (for the purpose of)...

⊙　用甚麼來維持生活？
What do you use to maintain your lifestyle?

(1)　政府用一家一個孩子的人口政策來控制人口。
The government employs the one-family-one-child policy to control population.

(2)　老師用考試的法子來逼學生念書。
The teacher uses examinations as a method to force students to study.

Excercises

一．完成對話　　(Complete the following dialogues with the expressions in parentheses.)

1.　A: 我不想在銀行工作，雖然這個工作能賺很多錢但是我對這個工作沒有興趣。

　　B: 我覺得賺錢最要緊，＿＿＿＿＿＿＿＿＿＿＿＿＿＿＿＿＿。

　　　　　　　　　　　　　　　　　　　（只要...就...）

2.　A: 為甚麼你覺得你的生活沒有意思？

　　B: ＿＿＿＿＿＿＿＿＿＿＿＿＿＿＿＿＿＿＿＿＿。

　　　　　　　　　　　　　　　　　　　（不是...就是...）

3.　A: 學期快結束的時候，學生都很忙嗎？

　　B: 是的，＿＿＿＿＿＿＿＿＿＿＿＿＿＿＿＿＿＿。

　　　　　　　　　　　　　　　　　　　（不是...就是...）

4.　A: 老師，這本書只看一次夠不夠？

　　B: ＿＿＿＿＿＿＿＿＿＿＿＿＿＿＿＿＿＿＿＿＿。

　　　　　　　　　　　　　　　　　　　（多 V）

5.　A: 我真想買車，可是車太貴了。

　　B: ＿＿＿＿＿＿＿＿＿＿＿＿＿＿＿＿＿＿＿＿＿？

　　　　　　　　　　　　　　　　　　　（只要 + rhetorical question）

二．翻譯　　　　(Translation)

1.　Ever since he graduated, he has mixed up with some bad friends. If they are not chatting then they are drinking. He does not have the skills to support his life.

2.　My parents oppose the idea of living together without getting married. Their way of thinking (concept) is out of date. In my view, as long as two people love each other, it doesn't matter whether they get married or not.

3.　She usually studies very late and won't go home until midnight. Because there are so many thefts and rapes on campus, her parents worry a great deal.

4.   How can a high school senior who has no skills live together with his girlfriend?

三．作文　　(Composition)

我對同居的看法。

第七課

信（三）

Vocabulary

墮胎 墮胎	duòtāi duohtai	VO:	to have an abortion; to perform an abortion
		N:	abortion
吸毒	xī-dú shi-dwu	VO:	"inhale poison", to use (illegal) drugs
使	shǐ shyy	V:	to make
委屈	wěiqū woeichiu	Adj: V: N:	(to feel) as if being treated unfairly; to feel frustrated or wronged unfair treatment (emotion)
懷孕 怀孕	huáiyùn hwaiyunn	VO:	to be pregnant
成爲 成为	chéngwéi cherngwei	V:	to become
避孕	bìyùn bihyunn	VO: N:	"avoid pregnancy", to prevent conception, to practice birth control contraception
方法	fāngfǎ fangfaa	N:	method
進步 进步	jìnbù jinnbuh	Adj:	advanced (in technology)
＿得很	de hěn de heen	Adv:	very (e.g., 好得很＝很好)
合法	héfǎ herfaa	Adj:	"in accord with the law", legal
手術 手术	shǒushù shooushuh	N:	operation, surgery
拔牙	bá-yá bar-ya	VO:	to extract a tooth

顆 顆	kē ke	M:	measure word for tooth or small round things
爲 为	wèi wey	Prep:	for (this reason)
真正	zhēnzhèng jenjenq	Adj:	real, true, actual
不是…而是…	bú.sh ... ér.sh bu.sh ... erl.sh		not ... but ...
負擔 负担	fùdān fuhdan	V: N:	to carry the burden of ... burden
找事	zhǎoshì jaoshyh	VO:	to look for a job
獨立 独立	dúlì dwulih	Adj:	"singly stand", independent
生孩子	shēng hái.zi sheng hairtz	VO:	to bear children, to have children
…也好…也好	A yě hǎo, B yě hǎo A yee hao, B yee hao		either A or B
主張 主张	zhǔzhāng juujang	V: N:	to propose, to advocate proposal
干涉	gānshè gansheh	V: N:	to interfere interference
提到	tídào tyidaw	V:	to mention
破案	pò-àn poh-ann	VO:	to clear up a case
原來 原来	yuánlái yuanlai	Adv:	(to realize the actual situation) it turned out that
據説 据说	jùshuō jiuhshuo		"It is said"
毒癮 毒瘾	dúyǐn dwuyiin	N:	addiction to drugs

發	发	fā fa		V:	to have a sudden onset of ...
毒品		dúpǐn dwupiin		N:	"poison items", drugs; narcotics
情形		qíng.xíng chyng.shyng		N:	situation
嚴重	严重	yánzhòng yanjonq		Adj:	serious in nature, grave
歲	岁	suì suey		N:	age
自由		zìyóu tzyhyou		N: Adj:	freedom free

Sentence Patterns

1. 使   to make; to cause (formal usage of 讓)

⊙   爸媽反對他跟女朋友住在一起，使他覺得很委屈。
His parents opposed his living together with his girlfriend, which caused him to feel he was treated unfairly.

(1)   他的教法使學生對這門課非常有興趣。
His method of teaching made the students very interested in this course.

(2)   你的樣子使我想起我小時候的情形。
Your appearance reminds me of my childhood days.

(3)   聽到這個壞消息使人很難過。
Hearing this bad news makes people very sad.

2. 再說   moreover; furthermore

⊙   懷孕的可能很小；再說就是懷了孕，墮胎也是合法的。
The chances of getting pregnant are very small; furthermore even if she were to get pregnant, abortion would still be legal.

(1)   A: 你為甚麼不選物理做專業呢？
A: Why don't you choose physics as your major ?

B: 我對物理沒有興趣，再說學物理不一定找得到工作，所以我不學物理。
B: I have no interest in studying physics. Furthermore, studying physics does not necessarily guarantee I can find a job; therefore I'm not studying physics.

(2)   A: 你不是說要買車的嗎？為甚麼又不買了呢？
A: Didn't you say that you wanted to buy a car ? Why didn't you buy one ?

B: 因為最近家裡沒有錢，再說我並不是真的需要用車所以我就不買了。

B: Because recently my family hasn't had any money; moreover, I don't really need a car. So, I didn't buy one.

(3) 那個房子真便宜,再說離你上班的地方又近,你還是買那個房子吧.

That house is really inexpensive; moreover it's also very near to where you work. You should really buy that house.

3. 就是 ... 也   even (if)   (intensive stressing a suppositional condition)

⊙ 就是懷了孕，墮胎也是合法的。

Even if she gets pregnant, abortion is still legal.

就是 + Verb Phrase + 也

(1) 現在找工作很難，就是大學畢業也不一定找得到工作。

It's difficult to find jobs nowadays. Even if you're a college graduate, that still doesn't guarantee you'll find a job.

(2) 就是你反對這件事我也要做。

Even if you oppose me in this matter, I will still do it.

(3) 就是給我很多的錢，我也不會到那儿去。

Even if (they) give me a lot of money, I still will not go there.

就是 + N + 也 = 連 + N + 也

(4) 就是小孩儿也看得懂這個字。
= 連小孩儿也看得懂這個字。

Even a small child can understand this word.

(5) 就是週末也得上班。
= 連週末也得上班。

Even on weekends (she) must go to work.

61

4.　**A 比 B 還**　　A is even more ... than B

⊙　這個手術比拔一顆牙還容易。
This operation is even easier than pulling a tooth.

(1)　從這儿到那儿去，走路比開車還快。
Walking from here to there is even quicker than driving.

(2)　有的時候小孩子比大人還聰明。
Sometimes a small child is even smarter than an adult.

(3)　聽說日文比中文還難，是真的嗎？
I've heard that Japanese is even harder than Chinese. Is it true?

A 比 B 更

(1)　我很高，他比我更高。
I'm very tall. He is even taller than me.

(2)　這間屋子亮，那間比這間更亮。
This room is bright. That one is even brighter than this one.

5.　**A 也好，B 也好**　　　　no matter whether A or B

⊙　要同居也好，要生孩子也好，那都是他自己的事。
Whether he wants to live with someone or have children, that is his own business.

(1)　這個房子是你的，你賣也好，送人也好，没有人會管你。
This house is yours, whether you sell it or give it away, no one will mind.

(2)　學生也好，老師也好，都不喜歡考試。
Be it students or teachers, no one likes exams.

(3)　城裡也好，鄉下也好，到處都是人。
Whether it's the city or the country, every place is crowded with people.

(4)　A: 這本書貴不貴？
A: Is this book expensive?
B: 貴也好，便宜也好，我都得買。
B: Whether it's expensive or cheap, I still must buy it.

Excercises

一．完成對話 (Complete the following dialogues with the expressions in parentheses)

1. A: 你為什麼大學畢業以後還跟父母住在一塊儿？

    B: _____ 。

    (...再說...)

2. A: 你為什麼不學那門課了？

    B: _____ 。

    (...再說...)

3. A: 什麼？你要跟男朋友同居，你難道不怕父母生氣？

    B: _____ 。

    (就是...也)

4. A: 要是那本書很貴，你還要買嗎？

    B: 對了，_____ 。

    (A也好，B也好)

5. A: 老師，今天我有一點不舒服，我可以不可以不考試？

    B: _____ 。

    (A也好，B也好)

6. A: 你對物理有興趣還是對化學有興趣？

    B: _____ 。

    (A也好，B也好)

二．翻譯 (Translation)

1. Some students feel that they are wronged because they are forced to take exams. However, whether they are forced (to take them) or volunteer (to take them), they still have to take them, since this is the best way for teachers to decide students' grades.

2. Even if parents do not advocate living together before marriage, they should not interfere when their children want to do so.

3. It's her (own) business whether she wants to have a child or have an abortion. It's no longer necessary for us to interfere with her freedom. She knows what she wants to do.

4. I am opposed to your making friends with him. He used to steal. Moreover, he has a bad drug habit. He is a person with serious problems.

5. Some people feel that using drugs should be legal. In their view, using drugs is the same as drinking (wine).

三．作文　　　(Composition)

吸毒在美國是不是一個很嚴重的問題？為甚麼？

第八課

信 （四）

Vocabulary

愛情 爱情	àiqíng aychyng	N:	love
大吃一驚 大吃一惊	dàchī'yì-jīng dahchy'i-jing		to be greatly startled (at ...)
類　類	lèi ley	M/N:	type, kind
看法	kànfǎ kannfaa	N:	viewpoint, view, opinion
竟	jìng jinq	Adv:	unexpectedly (emphatic), actually (contrary to assumption or expectation)
隨便 随便	suíbiàn sweibiann	Adj:	"follow-(one's)-convenience", casual, not serious
同意	tóngyì torngyih	V:	to agree (NOTE: This verb can only take an opinion as its object, i.e., DO NOT SAY 我跟你同意 or 我同意你）
殺人 杀人	shārén sharen	VO:	to kill people
在我看來 在我看来	zàiwǒkànlái tzay woo kann.lai		from my point of view
母體 母体	mǔtǐ muutii	N:	the mother's body
胎兒 胎儿	tāi'ér tai'erl	N:	fetus
生命	shēngmìng shengminq	N:	(physical) life

任何	rènhé rennher	Adj:	any
活下去	huó-xiàqù hwo-shiahchiuh	RV:	to continue to live
權利　权利	quánlì chyuanlih	N:	rights
就是	jiùshì jiow.sh		even
例外	lìwài lihway	V:	(to be) an exception an exception
換一句話説 换一句话说	huàn yí-jù huà shuō huann i-jiuh huah shuo		"change a sentence say", in other words
句	jù jiuh	M:	measure word for speech; sentence
隨意　随意	suíyì sweiyih	Adv:	"follow-intention", thoughtlessly, casually
殺害　杀害	shāhài shahay	V:	"kill-harm", kill
表示	biǎoshì beaushyh	V:	to express, to manifest (opinion, emotion, thanks, etc.)
理解	lǐjiě liijiee	V:	to understand, to comprehend
提醒	tíxǐng tyishiing	V:	to remind, to warn
努力　努力	nǔlì nuulih	Adj:	hardworking, diligent (NOTE: 努力 can be applied to any situation, 用功 is limited to academics, i.e., "to study hard")
建立	jiànlì jiannlih	RV:	to establish
幸福	xìngfú shinqfwu	Adj:	happy, fortunate (referring to family life)

66

家庭	jiātíng jiatyng	N:	family unit, household
責任 责任	zérèn tzerrenn	N:	responsibility
觀念 观念	guānniàn guanniann	N:	concept, idea
在…中	zài ... zhōng tzay ... jong	Prep:	in (formal)
找刺激	zhǎo-cìjī jao.tsyh.ji	VO:	to look for excitement
刺激	cìjī tsyh.ji	N: Adj:	excitement, stimulation; exciting exciting
作愛 作爱	zuòài tzuoh-ay	VO:	to make love (this is a straight translation from English)
自認 自认	zìrèn tzyhrenn	V:	to consider oneself as
保守	bǎoshǒu baoshoou	Adj:	conservative
值得	zhíde jyr.de	V:	to be worthwhile (for someone to do something)
參考 参考	cānkǎo tsankao	V:	to consult, to use as reference
地方	dìfāng dihfang	N:	part, aspect
勸 劝	quàn chiuann	V:	to urge, exhort, persuade, disuade
關於 关于	guānyú guanyu	Prep:	concerning, about
有意見 有意见	yǒu yìjiàn yeou yih.jiann	VO:	to have an opinion (here: a differing opinion), comments; to object
保羅 保罗	Bǎoluó Baoluo		Paul
學識 学识	xuéshì shyueshyh	N:	learning, erudition

人品	rénpǐn renpiin	N:	(moral) character
免不了	miǎnbù-liǎo mean.bu-leau	RV:	cannot avoid; it's inevitable that ...
將來 将来	jiānglái jianglai	TW: N:	in the future future
膚色 肤色	fūsè fuseh	N:	color of the skin
語言 语言	yǔyán yeuyan	N:	language
和	hé her	Conj:	and
文化	wénhuà wenhuah	N:	culture
背景	bèijǐng beyjiing	N:	background
差異 差异	chāyì cha'yih	N:	difference (formal)
社會 社会	shèhuì shehhuey	N:	society
受到歧視 受到歧视	shòudào qíshì showdaw chyishyh		to be discriminated against
歧視 歧视	qíshì chyishyh	V: N:	to discriminate discrimination
考慮 考虑	kǎolǜ kaoliuh	V:	to think over, to ponder, to take into consideration

Sentence Patterns

1. 竟然　　　surprisingly, unexpectedly

⊙ 真沒想到你對同居的看法竟是這麼隨便。
I certainly didn't expect that your view on living together would be so casual.

(1) 我的女朋友竟然跟別人結婚了。
My girlfriend unexpectedly married someone else.

(2) 你竟敢把我的車賣了，你真可惡！
You dare to sell my car! You're awful!

2. 把 A V 成 B

⊙ 你把墮胎說成比拔牙還容易。
You speak of abortion as being easier than pulling a tooth.

(1) 我把‘天’字看成‘大’字了。
I saw the character "tian" as the character "dah".

(2) 他把自己的經驗寫成一本書。
He took his own experiences and wrote a book from them.

(3) 我把三十塊錢聽成十三塊錢了。
I heard thirty dollars to be thirteen dollars.

(4) 學生把考試看成很可怕的事。
The students saw the test as a terrifying thing.

3. 在 ...看來 ， ...　　　in ...'s view

⊙ 墮胎跟殺人，在我看來，並沒有甚麼不同。
In my view, there is really no difference between abortion and murder.

(1) 在他看來 ...
In his view, ...

69

(2) 在中國人看來，...
From the point of view of Chinese, ...

(3) 在學過經濟的人看來，...
From the point of view of one who has studied economics, ...

4. 任何 A 都 B　　any; every; whatever ..... all ....

⊙ 任何人都有活下去的權利。
Everyone has the right to live.

(1) 我對任何文學的方面的書都有興趣。
I am interested in any book on literature.

(2) 任何人都希望生活過得好一點儿。
Every person hopes to live a better life.

(3) 他小的時候很笨，任何人都看不出來他會變成一個這麼有名的人。
He was very stupid when he was a child. Nobody could foresee that he would turn into such a famous person.

5. 關於　　　as for; concerning; in regard to

⊙ 關於你的男朋友我有一點儿意見。
I have some opinions (objections) concerning your boyfriend.

(1) 關於這件事，我們兩個人的看法不同。
Regarding this matter, we both have different opinions.

(2) 關於你自己的事，你應該自己決定。
As for your personal matters, you should decide for yourself.

(3) 關於歷史的書我都沒有興趣。
I have no interest in books concerning history.

(4) 他喜歡談關於政治的問題。
He likes to discuss issues that concern politics.

(5) 他買的書是關於中國歷史的。
The books he bought are about Chinese history.

(6) 我昨天看的電影是關於美國社會的。
The movie I saw yesterday was about American society.

(7) 我寫的報告是關於日本和中國的經濟關係的。
The paper I wrote was about Sino-Japanese economic relations.

6. 免不了　　　cannot avoid

⊙ 因為他是美國人，這免不了讓我對你們的將來有些擔心。
Because he is an American, this unavoidably causes me to have some concerns about your future.

(1) 你跟性情這麼奇怪的人結婚，免不了離婚。
Getting married to a person with such a strange disposition (temperment), you can't avoid getting a divorce.

(2) 朋友在一塊儿，吵架是免不了的。
When friends are together (for too long), arguments are unavoidable.

(3) 開快車免不了會出事。
Driving too fast will inevitably cause accidents.

Excercises

一．完成對話 (Complete the following dialogues with the expressions in parentheses.)

1.　A: 上個周末你看了什麼電影 (diànyǐng, movie)？

　　B: _____。
　　　　　　　　　　　　　　　　　　　　　　　　（關於）

2.　A: 你喜歡看什麼書？

　　B: _____。
　　　　　　　　　　　　　　　　　　　　　　　　（任何）

3.　A: 為什麼學生常常拉肚子？

　　B: _____。
　　　　　　　　　　　　　　　　　　　　　　　　（免不了）

4.　A: 他們的婚姻為什麼常常發生問題？

　　B: _____。
　　　　　　　　　　　　　　　　　　　　　　　　（免不了）

5.　A: 為什麼有很多中國人喜歡生男孩不喜歡生女孩？

　　B: _____。
　　　　　　　　　　　　　　　　　　　　　　　　（再說）

6.　A: 你要跟那個比你大二十歲的人結婚，父母一定會反對。

　　B: _____。
　　　　　　　　　　　　　　　　　　　　　　　　（就是...也）

7.　其實,在我看來,年紀 (age) 的差異不是最要緊的 _____

　　_____。
　　　　　　　　　　　　　　　　　　　　　　　　（只要...就...）

8. A: 我不相信他學了三年中文。

   B: 是啊，我也不相信。他說他學了三年中文可是 _____

   _____ 。
   （竟）

9. A: 下個星期誰得來上課？

   B: _____ 。
   （任何）

二．翻譯　(Translation)

1. My grandfather is from Japan. Although he has lived in America for 40 years, he doesn't consider himself to be an American.

2. Having different cultural backgrounds is not the issue. People with different cultural backgrounds can still establish a happy family.

3. People from different ethnic groups can still build a happy family if they get married. However, in the country, most people have a conservative view. If they want to live in the country, they can't avoid being discriminated against.

4. Due to the big difference in our language and cultural backgrounds, when we discuss questions we cannot avoid having different opinions.

5. People who oppose abortion say that everyone has the right to continue to live, even a fetus.

6. My parents are very conservative; their concepts are out of date. In their view, interfering with their children's love lives is their responsibility. They think they are parents who care for their children very much.

三．作文　(Composition)

在你看來，不同人種結婚會不會幸福，為什麼？

第九課

信（五）

Vocabulary

代溝 代沟	dàigōu daygou	N:	generation gap
女權 女权	nǚquán neuchyuan	N:	woman's rights
之間 之间	zhījiān jyjian		among, between
丈夫	zhàngfū janq.fu	N:	husband (also 先生, 愛人)
過去 过去	guòqù guochiuh	N:	for the past (year or period of time) the past
來 来	lái lai		the time up to the speaking moment
交往	jiāowǎng jiauwoang	V:	to have a relationship with a (girlfriend/boyfriend), to socialize with a (friend)
比較 比较	bǐjiào biijiaw	Adv: V:	comparatively, quite, rather to compare
待人	dàirén dayren	V:	to treat people
誠懇 诚恳	chéngkěn cherngkeen	Adj:	sincere(ly)
對…有信心 对…有信心	duì ... yǒu xìnxīn duey ...yeou shinnshin		to have confidence in ...
充滿 充满	chōngmǎn chongmaan	V:	to be filled with (abstract)
信心	xìnxīn shinnshin	N:	confidence

段	duàn duann	M:	a measure word for time, period
時期　时期	shíqī shyrchi		a period of time
説來説去 说来说去	shuō-lái shuō-qù shuo-lai shuo-chiuh		saying repeatedly
合適　合适	héshì hershyh	Adj:	suitable, appropriate
人種　人种	rénzhǒng renjoong	N:	race
不必	búbì bubih	Adv:	need not
事業　事业	shìyè shyhyeh	N:	professional career
婚事	hūnshì huenshyh	N:	marriage
待	daī dai	V:	to stay
看	kān kan	V:	to look after (children)
管	guǎn goan	V:	to be in charge of
家事	jiāshì jiashyh	N:	housework
過時　过时	guòshí guohshyr	V:	out of date, out of fashion
抱不平	bàobùpíng bawbupyng	V:	"to hold unfairness", to feel indignant
一輩子　一辈子	yíbèizi i-beytz	N:	(one's) whole life, a whole lifetime
煮飯　煮饭	zhǔ-fàn juu-fann	VO:	"boil rice", to cook
打掃　打扫	dǎsǎo daasao	V:	to tidy, to clean up

過 过	gùo guoh	V:	to live
單調 单调	dāndiào dandiaw	Adj:	monotonous
無聊 无聊	wúliáo wuliau	Adj:	boring
部份	bùfèn buhfenn	N:	part, section
犧牲 牺牲	xīshēng shisheng	V:	to sacrifice
暫時 暂时	zhànshí jannshyr	Adv:	for the time being

Sentence Patterns

1. 對 ... 有 信 心　　　to have confidence in .....

⊙ 他對將來充滿信心。
He is filled with confidence about his future.

(1) 我現在對說中文有信心了。
I now have the confidence to speak in Chinese.

(2) 他對自己一點儿也沒有信心。
He has no confidence in himself whatsoever.

(3) 你對你的將來有沒有信心？
Do you have any confidence in your future?

2. V 來 V 去

to do the action repeatedly or for a long time

⊙ 爸說來說去就因為保羅是美國人，所以跟我結婚不合適。
Father kept saying that because Paul is American, he is not suitable for me to marry.

(1) 我看來看去都看不出來這是誰寫的字。
After looking at this over and over, I still can't make out whose writing this is.

(2) 他說來說去我還是沒聽懂。
After he said it over and over, I still couldn't understand.

(3) 那本書我找來找去都找不到。
I looked high and low for that book but still couldn't find it.

(4) 我看來看去總算看出來是誰寫的字了。
After looking at this repeatedly, I finally figured out who wrote it.

(5) 他說來說去，我終於聽懂了。
After he said it over and over, I finally understood.

(6) 那本書我找來找去最後在圖書館找到了。
After searching high and low for that book, I finally found it in the library.

3. 為   for

⊙ 為這個問題顧慮。
(I) am concerned about this issue.

(1) 我為沒有受過良好教育的人抱不平。
I feel indignant at the injustice suffered by people who don't receive a good education.

(2) 我不為他抱不平。
I don't feel any indignation for him.

(3) 你為不為他抱不平？
Do you feel any indignation for him?

(4) 他為國家犧牲了生命。
He sacrificed his life for his country.

(5) 政府應該為老百姓服務。
The government should serve the people.

(6) 我真為你的病擔心。
I am really concerned about your illness.

4. 先 V1 再 V2   first V1 then (after ...) V2

⊙ 我很想先做幾年事，等自己在事業上有了一些成績以後再談婚事。
I want to work for a few years first. After I become successful in my career then I will discuss marriage.

(1) 你可以先洗菜，等客人來了以後再切。
You can wash the vegetables first and then after the guests arrive cut them.

(2)　我想先念大學，等大學畢業再找事。
I want to first study in college. After I graduate then I'll look for a job.

5.　在 ... 上　　　　　　in the aspect of (in abstract sense); in terms of ... ; as far as ...

⊙　他同意：在經濟上不能獨立以前，暫時不談跟女朋友同居的事。
He agreed that, before he is economically independent, he would not talk about living with his girlfriend for the time being.

(1)　在經濟上，紐約是一個非常重要的地方。
Economically, New York is a very important place.

(2)　在學習上，他非常努力。
In studies, he is very diligent.

Excercises

一．完成對話　　(Complete the following dialogues with the expressions in parentheses.)

1.　A: 現在在美國多半儿的學生都一畢業就結婚嗎？

　　B: _____。
　　　　　　　　　　　　　　　　　　　　　　　　（先...再...）

2.　A: 你的照相機找到了沒有？

　　B: _____。
　　　　　　　　　　　　　　　　　　　　　　　　（V來V去）

3.　A: 你想選什麼專業？

　　B: _____。
　　　　　　　　　　　　　　　　　　　　　　　　（V來V去）

二．翻譯　　　　(Translation)

1.　A:　I feel that my life is not only boring but also monotonous.
　　B:　Given the fact that you are so unhappy, why don't you go traveling to foreign countries?

2.　I am fully confident of my future. I believe that as long as I work hard and treat people sincerely I will definitely achieve success in my career.

3.　The idea that women should only stay at home cooking and taking care of children is out of date. Nowadays, women can be like men. They can have their own careers.

4.　I have been dating Mr. Wang for three years. We share the same interests in Chinese language and culture. However, since I am only 18 years old now, we haven't talked about getting married yet.

5.　Inter-racial marriage is not uncommon now. Whether he (or she) is sincere or not is much more important than which race he (or she) belongs to.

三、作文　　(Composition)

1. Continue the following dialogue using your own imagination. The following words must be used : to be pregnant, not serious, a happy family, in one's view, to have control, responsibility.

    A:　我們已經同居了兩年了，...
    B:　...

2. 小芬 is going to marry Paul（保羅）. Paul is now trying to get 小芬's father to consent to their marriage. Please write a dialogue between Paul and 小芬's father (at least 10 sentences). The following expressions must be used: prejudice, to be descriminated against, to sacrifice, generation gap.

第 十 課

五 封 信 的 討 論

Vocabulary

討論 讨论	tǎolùn taoluenn	V: N:	to discuss discussion
甲	jiǎ jea	Pro:	the first of the ten Heavenly Stems here used to refer to the first person in the conversation
作者	zuòzhě tzuohjee	N:	author
淺 浅	qiǎn chean	Adj:	shallow
成見 成见	chéngjiàn cherngjiann	N:	"fixed opinion", a prejudice
既…又…	jì … yòu jih … yow		both … and …
代表	dàibiǎo daybeau	V:	to express, to illustrate, to manifest
表現 表现	biǎoxiàn beaushiann	N:	manifestation; expression
偏見 偏见	piānjiàn pianjiann	N:	"inclined opinion", bias, prejudice
幼稚	yòuzhì yowjyh	Adj:	naive; childish, puerile
處處 处处	chùchù chuhx	PW:	everywhere
尊重	zūnzhòng tzuenjonq	V:	to respect
女性	nǚxìng neushinq	N:	female

82

大男人主義 大男人主义	dà'nánrén zhǔyì dahnanren juuyih	N:	male chauvinism, also known as 大男子主義
主義　主义	zhǔyì juuyih	N:	-ism
色情	sèqíng sehchyng	N: Adj:	pornography pornographic
暴力	bàolì bawlih	N:	violence
引起···的興趣 引起···的兴趣	yǐnqǐ ... .de xìngqù yiinchii ... .de shinqchiuh	VO:	to attract ... interest
無聊　无聊	wúliáo wuliao	Adj:	senseless, silly
做法	zuòfǎ tzuohfaa	N:	way of doing ex: 說法, 寫法, 唱法
推銷　推销	tuīxiāo tueishiau	V:	"push sale", to promote (sales)
産品　产品	chǎnpǐn chaanpiin	N:	products
用不着	yòngbù-zháo yonq.bu-jaur	RV:	need not
電視　电视	diànshì diannshyh	N:	television
廣告　广告	guǎnggào goanggaw	N:	TV commercials, advertisement
辦法　办法	bànfǎ bannfaa	N:	method
教材	jiàocái jiawtsair	N:	teaching materials
乙	yǐ yii	Pro:	the second of the ten Heavenly stems, here refers to the second person in the conversation
僞君子　伪君子	wěijūnzǐ woeijiuntzyy	N:	"false gentleman", hypocrite

打開	打开	dǎkāi daakai	V:	to open
報紙	报纸	bàozhǐ bawjyy	N:	newspaper
正		zhèng jenq	Adv:	precisely, exactly
結合	结合	jiéhé jyeher	V:	to tie together
極端	极端	jíduān jyiduan	Adj: N:	extreme an extreme
故事		gùshì guh.shyh	N:	story
至於	至于	zhìyú jyhyu		as for ...
說明	说明	shuōmíng shuoming	V: N:	to explain explanation
現代	现代	xiàndài shiannday	Adj:	modern
醫學	医学	yīxué ishyue	N:	medical science
安全		ānquán anchyuan	Adj: N:	safe safety
不見得	不见得	bújiàndé bujiannder		not necessarily
能力		nénglì nenglih	N:	ability
限制		xiànzhì shiannjyh	N: V:	restriction to restrict
膚淺	肤浅	fūqiǎn fuchean	Adj:	"skin-shallow", superficial, shallow, skin-deep
毛病		máobìng maubinq	N:	defect, flaw
課本	课本	kèběn kehbeen	N:	textbooks

哲學 哲学	zhéxué jershyue	N: philosophy
答案	dáàn dar'ann	N: an answer
生字	shēngzì shengtzyh	N: new words
句型	jùxíng jiuhshyng	N: sentence patterns

Sentence Patterns

1. 既 ... 又 / 也   not only ... but also; both ... and ...

⊙   這些看法既不能代表中國人，又不能代表美國人。
These viewpoints can represent neither Chinese nor Americans.

(1)   坐飛機既安全又舒服。
Flying in a plane is both safe and comfortable.

(2)   王先生既不喜歡抽煙又不喜歡喝酒。
Mr. Wang likes neither smoking nor drinking.

2. 引起 ... 的 N   to draw out; to arouse; to attract

⊙   作者想用色情跟暴力的題目來引起學生的興趣。
The author wants to use sex and violence as topics to arouse the students'
interest.

(1)   為了引起人們看電影的興趣，電影裡充滿了色情
跟暴力。
In order to draw viewers' interest to watching movies, the movies
are filled with pornography and violence.

(2)   小孩儿哭是為了引起大人的注意。
Children cry to draw adults' attention (to them).

(3)   那隻受傷的小狗引起了大家的同情。
That injured puppy gained everyone's sympathy.

3. 用不著   do not have to; unnecessary

⊙   用不著拿電視廣告的辦法來刺激學生。
It is not necessary to use TV commercials as a way to stimulate students.

(1)   你用不著生氣，他已經跟你道歉了。
You needn't be angry. He has already apologized to you.

(2) 你自己決定吧，用不著跟大家討論了。
You decide it for yourself. You don't need to discuss it with everyone.

(3) 我的病不嚴重，用不著看大夫。
My illness is not serious. I don't need to see a doctor.

(4) 這本書我用不著了，送給你吧。
I don't need this book anymore. I'll give it to you.

(5) 這儿的天氣真熱，冬天的衣服都用不著。
The weather here is really hot. (You) don't need any winter clothes.

(6) 要是用得著就買吧，貴不貴沒關係。
If it's useful then buy it. Whether it's expensive or not doesn't matter.

4. 再也不　　　emphasizes that something will never be repeated

⊙ 我希望再也不要看到這樣的教材了。
I hope I will never see this kind of teaching material again.

(1) 他總是騙人，我再也不會相信他了。
He is always lying. I will never believe him again.

(2) 這家飯館的服務真差，我再也不來了。
This restaurant's service is really bad. I will never come here again.

(3) 他到美國去了以後再也沒回來過。
After he went to America, he never came back again.

(4) 再也別買這種糖了，又貴又難吃。
Don't buy this kind of candy again. It's expensive and tastes bad.

5. 把 A 跟 B 結合起來　　　to tie A and B together

⊙ 拿這樣的題目做教材，正是把學習跟生活結合起來。
Using these kinds of issues as teaching materials actually ties studies and life together.

(1) 把經驗跟知識結合起來。
[] integrates experience and knowledge

(2)　　把工作跟生活結合起來。
[] ties one's job and life together.

6.　才 ... （呢）　　emphasizes contradiction of the previous statement

⊙　如果每個故事都只是教我們做好人、做好事，那才無聊呢！
If every story only teaches us to be good people, and to do good things, that's just boring!

(1)　A: 你真笨。
　　A: You're really stupid.

　　B: （我不笨，）你才笨呢。
　　B: (I'm not stupid,) you're the stupid one.

(2)　A: 看電視真有意思。
　　A: Watching TV is really interesting.

　　B: 看電視沒有意思，看電影才有意思呢。
　　B: Watching TV is not interesting, watching a movie is interesting.

(3)　物理我不喜歡，歷史才是我喜歡的。
　　I don't like physics, it's history that I like.

7.　至於　　as for ...

⊙　至於墮胎比拔牙還容易 ...。
As for abortion being easier than pulling a tooth ... .

(1)　我去過北京、上海；至於台北，我還沒去過。
　　I've been to Peking and Shanghai, but as for Taipei, I still haven't been there yet.

(2)　A:　你今年住在這兒，明年呢？
　　A:　This year you live here, (but) what about next year?

　　B:　今年我打算住在這兒，至於明年住在哪兒，我還沒決定。

B: This year I plan to live here, (but) as for next year, I still haven't decided.

(3) 我剛找到一份工作，至於工作有沒有意思我還不知道。
I just found a job, but as for whether the job is interesting or not, I still don't know.

8. 受到 ... 的（限制，歧視，影響，注意）

to receive (in an abstract sense)

⊙ 因為（受到）語言能力的限制，在討論問題的時候...。
Because they are restricted in their ability to use the language, when discussing issues ... .

(1) 因為受到政府的限制，外國人不能到中國的鄉下去旅行。
Because they have been restricted by the government, foreigners cannot travel through the Chinese countryside.

(2) 在美國，女人在社會上是不是受到很大的歧視？
In America, do women feel a great deal of prejudice in society?

(3) 因為受到我朋友的影響，我也開始抽煙了。
Because I was influenced by my friend, I also started smoking.

(4) 這件事受到了大家的注意。
This issue has received everyone's attention.

= 大家都注意這件事。
Everyone pays attention to this issue.

Excercises

一．完成對話

(Complete the following dialogues with the expressions in parentheses.)

1.　A: 你為甚麼要選這門課？

　　B: ＿＿＿＿＿＿＿＿＿＿＿＿＿＿＿＿＿＿ 。
　　　　　　　　　　　　　　　　　　（既⋯又⋯）

2.　A: 這兩個人的意見你都同意嗎？

　　B: ＿＿＿＿＿＿＿＿＿＿＿＿＿＿＿＿＿＿ 。
　　　　　　　　　　　　　　　　　　（既⋯又⋯）

3.　A: 你昨天是不是跟你的同屋吵架了？

　　B: ＿＿＿＿＿＿＿＿＿＿＿＿＿＿＿＿＿＿ 。
　　　　　　　　　　　　　　　　　　（再也不）

4.　A: 那家飯館的飯又貴又不好吃，你還想去嗎？

　　B: ＿＿＿＿＿＿＿＿＿＿＿＿＿＿＿＿＿＿ 。
　　　　　　　　　　　　　　　　　　（再也不）

5.　A: 明年跟後年你有甚麼計劃？

　　B: ＿＿＿＿＿＿＿＿＿＿＿＿＿＿＿＿＿＿ 。
　　　　　　　　　　　　　　　　　　（⋯至於⋯）

6.　A: 今年夏天你的計劃是到北京去，明年夏天呢？

　　B: ＿＿＿＿＿＿＿＿＿＿＿＿＿＿＿＿＿＿ 。
　　　　　　　　　　　　　　　　　　（至於）

7.　A: 高中畢業的人可以不可以在高中教書？

　　B: ＿＿＿＿＿＿＿＿＿＿＿＿＿＿＿＿＿＿ 。
　　　　　　　　　　　　　　　　　　（才⋯呢）

8.　A: 你的老師喜歡怎麼教中文？

　　B: ＿＿＿＿＿＿＿＿＿＿＿＿＿＿＿＿＿＿ 。
　　　　　　　　　　　　　　　　　　（用⋯來⋯）

二. 翻譯 (Translation)

1. In my view, promoting a product with television commercials is not necessarily useful.

2. Some parents do not let their children watch T.V. because television is flooded with sex and violence. I think this kind of thinking is too extreme.

3. In class the teacher explains new words and the usage of sentence patterns.

4. A: Your opinion is not only shallow but also naive. I don't want to discuss questions with you any more.
   B: You are prejudiced against me. You are a male chauvinist pig (豬, ju, zhū) who does not respect women.

5. You are really a hypocrite. You say that you respect women, but actually you are a male chauvinist.

6. Not only does this teaching material integrate learning with living, moreover, the new words and sentence patterns are very useful.

7. In order to draw people's interest to watching TV, TV programs are filled with pornography and violence.

8. People who oppose the use of these teaching materials say that the opinions expressed in them are too extreme. In fact, these types of materials integrate study with everyday life, and draw students' interest to further discussion.

9. We do not discriminate against women and people from different cultures; as long as you have experience you will have no problem applying for this job.

10. He thinks that combining life and study is a good way to arouse students' interest.

三. 作文 (Composition)

1. 在你看來，甚麼教材是對學生最有幫助的教材？

第十一課

到 中 國 去

Vocabulary

飛機 飞机	fēijī feiji	N: airplane
乘客	chéngkè cherngkeh	N: passenger
對話 对话	duìhuà dueyhuah	N: dialogue
同志	tóngzhì torngjyh	N: comrade
准　准	zhǔn joen	V: to allow, to permit
抽烟	chōu-yān chou-ian	VO: "inhale smoke", to smoke
位子	wèizi weytz	N: seat
關你什麼事 关你什么事	guān nǐ shén(.me) shì guan nii sherm(.me) shyh	What business is it of yours?
咳嗽	késòu ker.sow	V: to cough
聞　闻	wén wen	V: to smell
味儿 味儿	wèr well	N: a smell; a taste
講理 讲理	jiǎnglǐ jeanglii	Adj: "talk-reason", reasonable
廣播 广播	guǎngbō goangbo	V: to announce over a loudspeaker, to bradcast

各位	gè-wèi geh-wey		"every person", everybody (conventional way of beginning an announcement, equivalent to "Ladies and Gentlemen, ...")
旅客	lǚkè leukeh	N:	passenger
降落	jiàngluò jianqluoh	V:	to land (airplane)
機場　机场	jīchǎng jichaang	N:	airport
海關　海关	hǎiguān haeguan	N:	customs
申報單　申报单	shēnbàodān shenbawdan	N:	declaration form
趕快　赶快	gǎnkuài gaankuay	Adv:	hurry up
停穩　停稳	tíng-wěn tyng-woen	RV:	"to stop and be stabilized", to come to a complete stop
繫　系	jì jih	V:	to fasten
安全帶　安全带	ānquándài anchyuanday	N:	safety belt
安全	ānquán anchyuan	Adj: N:	safe safety
座位	zuòwèi tzuohwey	N:	seat (formal)
國際　国际	guójì gwojih	Adj:	international
客人	kèrén kehren	N:	guest
飯店　饭店	fàndiàn fanndiann	N:	hotel
司機　司机	sījī syji	N:	driver (as an occupation)

付	fù fuh	V:	to pay (a bill for something)
人民幣　人民币	rénmínbì renminbih	N:	"people's" currency, RMB
外匯券　外汇券	wàihuìquàn wayhueychiuann	N:	foreign exchange certificate
啦	la .la		a contraction of 了 and 啊
打折	dǎ.zhé daa-jer	VO:	to have a discount
收據　收据	shōujù shoujiuh	N:	receipt
上車　上车	shàngchē shanqche	VO:	to get into a car
出租汽車 出租汽车	chūzūqìchē chutzuchihche	N:	"out-rent-car", a cab, a taxi
租	zū tzu	V:	to rent
熟	shú (shóu) shwu (shour)	Adj:	to be familiar
故意	gùyì guhyih	Adv:	intentionally, on purpose, deliberately
繞路　绕路	rào-lù raw-luh	VO:	make a detour, take the long route 路 : road
修	xiū shiou	V:	to construct (a road, house, bridge, etc.), to repair
噢，是嗎 噢，是吗	Oh, shìma Oh, shyh.ma		Oh, is it so?
對⋯熟悉 对⋯熟悉	duì ... shúxi duey ... shwu.shi		to be familiar with ...
挺	tǐng tiing	Adv:	very, quite
前幾次　前几次	qiánjǐcì chyanjiitsyh	TW:	the last several times

辦事 办事	bàn-shì bann-shyh	VO:	handle business
上下班時間 上下班时间	shàng-xià-bān shíjiān shanq-shiah-ban shyrjian	TW:	"time of going and getting off work", rush hour
下班	xià-bān shiah-ban	VO:	to get off work
堵車 堵车	dǔ-chē duu-che		"to block automobiles", to have a traffic jam
根本	gēnběn genbeen	Adv:	simply, ... at all
走不動 走不动	zǒubu-dòng tzoou.bu-donq	RV:	"walk-not-move", cannot move
急事	jíshì jyishyh	N:	urgent business
多少	duōshǎo duoshao		how many, how much
算	suàn suann		to be considered as, to count as
小費 小费	xiǎofèi sheaufey	N:	"small fee", tip (NOTE: There is no such saying as "a big tip" in Chinese. The proper modifier is 多 not 大) 給小費: to tip
講　讲	jiǎng jeang	V:	"to talk about", to take seriously, to pay attention to, (e.g., "all they talked about is ..."), to promote
革命	gémìng germinq	N: V:	revolution to revolt
社會主義 社会主义	shèhuì zhǔyì shehhuey juuyih	N:	socialism
可	kě kee	Adv:	an adverb used to emphasize the verb or adjective followed

規矩 規矩	guījǔ guei.jeu	N:	rule, regulation, (here) social etiquette
		Adj:	well-behaved
找錢 找钱	zhǎo-(qián) jao-(chyan)	VO:	"to look for (small) money", to give change
行李	xínglǐ shyng.lii	N: (M:	luggage, baggage 件, e.g.: 一件行李)
提	tí tyi	V:	to carry by handle, to carry (in one's hand with arm down)
行李箱	xínglǐxiāng shyng.liishiang	N:	"luggage box", trunk (of a car)
蓋子 盖子	gàizi gaytz	N:	a cover, lid
堵	dǔ duu	V:	to block
旅館 旅馆	lǚguǎn leugoan	N:	hotel
訂房間 订房间	dìng-fángjiān dinq-farngjian	VO:	to reserve a room
查	chá char	V:	to check; to look up
記録 记录	jìlù jihluh	N: V:	a (written) record to make a (written) record
記错 记错	jì-cuò jih-tsuoh	RV:	to remember or record incorrectly
難道 难道	nándào nandaw	Adv:	Do you mean to say that ...?
訂單 订单	dìngdān dinqdan	N:	order slip, reservation slip
空房	kòng fáng konq farng	N:	unoccupied room, available room
麻煩 麻烦	máfán mafarn	V: Adj:	to trouble, to bother troublesome; inconvenient
洗澡	xǐ-zǎo shii-tzao	VO:	to take a bath, a shower

人民	rénmín renmin	N:	people
還是　还是	háishì hairshyh	Adv:	had better
倒霉	dǎoméi daomei	Adj: VO:	unfortunate (situation) to meet with misfortune (also written as 倒楣)
剛才　刚才	gāngcái gangtsair	TW:	a moment ago, just now
服務員　服务员	fúwùyuán fwuwuhyuan	N:	service personnel
服務　服务	fúwù fwuwuh	V: N:	to serve service
服務台　服务台	fúwùtái fwuwuhtair	N:	service desk
差	chà chah	Adj:	bad
吵	chǎo chao	Adj:	noisy
髒　脏	zāng tzang	Adj:	dirty
床單　床单	chuángdān chwangdan	N:	bed sheets
被子	bèizi beytz	N:	quilt
枕頭套　枕头套	zhěntóutào jeen.tourtaw	N:	pillowcase
枕頭　枕头	zhěntóu jeen.tour	N:	pillow
蟑螂	zhāngláng janglang	N:	cockroach
派	pài pay	V:	to send, to assign (a person)
天氣　天气	tiānqì tian.chih	N:	weather

冬天	dōngtiān dongtian	N:	winter
換 换	huàn huann	V:	to change; to exchange
態度 态度	tàidù tay.duh	N:	attitude
簡直 简直	jiǎnzhí jeanjyr	Adv:	simply too ...
不像話 不像话	búxiànghuà bushianqhuah	Adj:	"not resemble speech", uncalled for, unseemly, outrageous
帝國主義 帝国主义	dìguó zhǔyì dihgwo juuyih	N:	imperialism
嘴臉 嘴脸	zuǐliǎn tzoeilean	N:	"mouth and face", countenance (derogatory)
出錢 出钱	chū-qián chu-chyan	VO:	to pay, to contribute money
發脾氣 发脾气	fā-píqì fa-p̄yi.chih	VO:	to lose (one's) temper
他媽的 他妈的	tā māde ta mha.de	Intj:	damn it! damn ...

Sentence Patterns

1.　打 折

打 (number) 折 means "marked down to X% of the original price". This verb requires special attention because it is used in a sense opposite to its English equivalent. In other words the number between 打 and 折 refers to the amount remaining to be paid on a certain item after the discount.

⊙　打個九折是二十七塊錢。
A 10% discount makes it twenty-seven dollars.

(1)　打三折
mark 70% off

(2)　打九折
mark 10% off

(3)　打八五折
mark 15% off

(4)　打對折
mark half off

2.　A 對 B 熟 (悉)　　　A is familiar with B

⊙　你好像對北京挺熟悉的。
You seem to be quite familiar with Peking.

(1)　因為我剛來所以對這儿的情形不熟悉。
Because I have just arrived, I am not familiar with the situation here.

(2)　你對中國人的生活習慣熟悉不熟悉？
Are you familiar with the customs of daily life of Chinese people?

3. 從來不 / 没 V 過 (have) never V-ed (up to the point of speaking)

⊙ 前幾次來，從來没聽說過要給小費的。
The last few times I came here, I never heard that one had to give a tip.

(1) 他從來不在外頭吃飯（因為他覺得外頭的飯不乾淨）。
He never eats out (because he feels that the food outside is not clean).

(2) 他從來没在外頭吃過飯（他很想試試看）。
He has never eaten out (but he really wants to try it).

(3) 我最討厭喝這種汽水，所以我從來不喝。
I hate to drink this kind of soda the most, so I never drink it.

(4) 我從來没喝過這種汽水，今天是第一次喝。
I have never had this kind of soda. Today is my first time drinking it.

4. 可 adverb which acts as an intensifier

⊙ 以前中國人講革命，現在可不講了。
In the past, the Chinese people talked about revolution, but now they don't talk about it anymore.

(1) A: 他住的房子大不大？
A: Is the house he lives in large?

B: 他住的房子可大了，有十個房間。
B: He lives in a really big house. There are 10 rooms.

(2) 我累死了，我可不想去，你一個人去吧。
I'm dead tired. I certainly don't want to go. Why don't you go by yourself.

5. 難道 ...（嗎） Could it be ...?　　　Do you mean ...?

⊙ 我自己的名字難道還不知道嗎？
Do you mean to say that I don't know my own name?

(1) 他是你最好的朋友，難道他會騙你嗎？
He is your best friend. Do you mean to say that he would lie to you?

(2) 你怎麼連"大"字也不會寫，你難道没學過中文嗎？
How come you can't even write the character "dà"? Do you mean to say that you've never studied Chinese?

(3) 為甚麼他不跟我說話，難道他不喜歡我了？
Why doesn't he speak to me? Could it be that he doesn't like me?

6．才 indicates an action has just taken place, not long ago

⊙ 床單，被子是昨天才換的。
The sheets and blanket were just changed yesterday.

(1) 我是前天才來的，所以對這儿還不熟悉。
I didn't get here until two days ago, so I'm still not familiar with this place.

(2) 這個字你怎麼才學過就忘了。
How could you forget this word that you've just learned?

7．要 V 就 V，不 V 就 不 V
If you want to V, then V, if you don't want to V, then don't V

⊙ 你要住就住，不住就不住。
If you want to live there, then live there, if you don't want to live there, then don't live there.

(1) 要吃就吃，不吃就不吃。
If you want to eat, then eat, if you don't want to eat then don't eat.

(2) 你要買就買，不買就不買。
If you want to buy it then buy it, if you don't want to buy it, then don't buy it.

Excercises

一．完成對話　　(Complete the following dialogues with the expressions in parentheses.)

1. A: 聽說在那家飯館吃飯很貴，是真的嗎？

   B: _____。
   　　　　　　　　　　　　　　　　　　　（根本）

2. A: 喂，你好，這是人民旅館。

   B: _____。
   　　　　　　　　　　　　　　　　　　　（訂）

3. A: 他昨天告訴我他一定會來上課，結果他沒來，真奇怪！

   B: _____。
   　　　　　　　　　　　　　　　　　　　（難道）

4. A: 對一年級的學生，說中文很難，對不對？

   B: 對了，因為_____。
   　　　　　　　　　　　　　　　　　　　（才：just）

5. A: 在這個學校，一、二年級跟三、四年級的學生都得住在學校嗎？

   B: 不是，_____。
   　　　　　　　　　　　　　　　　　　　（才）

6. A: 在北京飯店，夏天有熱水嗎？

   B: 夏天沒有熱水，_____。
   　　　　　　　　　　　　　　　　　　　（才）

7. A: 紐約你去過嗎？

   B: 我從來沒去過所以_____

   _____。
   　　　　　　　　　　　　　　　　　　（對...熟）

8. A: 你的宿舍的房間怎麼樣？

   B: 簡直太差了，_____。
   　　　　　　　　　　　　　　　　　（不但...而且...）

9. A: 你昨天買的東西貴不貴？

B: 本來是100塊錢 _____

_____ 所以我只花了90塊錢。

（打折）

二．翻譯　　（Translation）

1. In a socialist country, because there are no customs for giving tips, service workers' attitudes are very bad.

2. In half an hour it will be rush hour. This road from the airport to the hotel is especially busy. Cars can't move at all. Therefore taxi drivers often lose their tempers.

3. This quilt and these sheets are both a bit dirty. Can you mark 20% off?

4. He purposely smokes in a no-smoking area. He's really ill-mannered (unreasonable).

5. Sorry, you've come too late to get (reserve) a room. Our rooms are all occupied (no vacant rooms). Go to the Empire (Imperial) Hotel.

6. A: "Eat it if you want. If you don't want it, don't eat it."
    B: "Don't lose your temper. I just had lunch. I'm not hungry."

7. Please give that hotel a call and ask them if they have any vacant rooms.

8. That driver's attitude is very bad. I gave him a five-dollar tip but he still wanted me to carry my luggage myself.

9. While the airplane is landing, every passenger has to fasten his seatbelt. No one is allowed to go to the bathroom.

10. I told the "service person" in the People's Hotel that the sheets and pillowcases had already been used and were very dirty. But he said that they had just been changed this morning. (use 才)

11. Do you mean to say that he will not remember his name if he smokes a cigarette?

12. In America, no passenger will be allowed to smoke on an airplane after February.

13. There is always a lot of traffic from the airport to the hotel, especially during rush hour. I heard that another road is going to be built soon.

14. Tipping is an American custom. Many Chinese who have just arrived in the country find that tipping is annoying.

三．作文　　　(Composition)

1.　Write a letter to a hotel manager to complain about the bad service in the hotel.

Describe your experiences in detail.

2.　Write a dialogue.

In your dialogue the following expressions must be used: (to reserve a room, service attitude, socialism, imperialism, to tip, to check).

第十二課

中國青年的煩惱

Vocabulary

青年	qīngnián chingnian	N:	youth, young people
煩惱　烦恼	fánnǎo farnnao	V: N:	to worry a vexation, a worry
市場　市场	shìchǎng shyhchaang	N:	market
斤	jīn jin	N:	catty, (now) kilogram
兩塊五　两块五	liǎng-kuài wǔ leang-kuay wuu	N:	two dollars and fifty cents
漲價　涨价	zhǎng-jià jaang-jiah	VO:	"rise price", price goes up
五毛	wǔ-máo wuu-mau	N:	fifty cents
屬害　厉害	lìhài lih.hay	Adj:	severe
自由市場 自由市场	zìyóu shìcháng tzyhyou shyhchaang	N:	free market
自由	zìyóu tzyhyou	Adj: N:	free freedom
唉	hài hay		sighing sound
過日子　过日子	guò-rìzi guoh-ryhtz	VO:	"pass the days", to live everyday life
日子	rìzi ryhtz	N:	day; specific date; life

105

可不是嗎 可不是吗	kěbúshì ma keebushyh .ma		Isn't that the way it is? (That's just the way it is.), "Ain't that the truth!"
柴	chái chair	N:	fuel, firewood
米	mǐ mii	N:	rice
油	yóu you	N:	oil
鹽　盐	yán yán	N:	salt
做生意	zuò-shēngyì tzuoh-sheng.yih	VO:	to do business
殺　杀	shā sha	V:	to kill (here): to kill and clean
弄	nòng nonq	V:	(colloquial) to do
老張　老张	Lǎo Zhāng Lao Jang		name
請客　请客	qǐng-kè chiing-keh	V:	to invite guests, to have a (dinner) party; to treat to (meal, movie, ...)
阿毛	Ā máo Ah mau		name
他們倆　他们俩	tāmén liǎ ta.men lea	N:	those two (倆 is a contracted form of 兩個人)
早	zǎo tzao	Adv:	long ago
單位　单位	dānwèi danwey	N:	unit, (work) unit
他倆　他俩	tā liǎ ta lea	N:	those two (further contraction of 他們倆)
北大	Běidà Beeidah	N:	Peking University (short for 北京大學)

幸運 幸运	xìngyùn shinqyunn	Adj:	lucky, fortunate
同一個 同一个	tóng yíge torng ig	N:	the same one
夫婦 夫妇	fūfù fufuh	N:	a married couple, husband and wife
分配	fēnpèi fenpey	V:	"allocate-match", (here) to assign (to a job); to divide
難得 难得	nándé nander	Adv: Adj:	seldom difficult to get (the chance to); precious (occasion)
見面 见面	jiàn-miàn jiann-miann	VO:	"see-face", to see someone, to meet someone (prearranged) (NOTE: 我見面你 is WRONG; 跟 must be used; e.g., 我跟你見面)
批准	pīzhǔn pijoen	V: N:	to approve, to permit approval, permission
主要	zhǔyào juuyaw	Adv: Adj:	primarily primary, most important
破	pò poh	Adj:	broken, worn out, bad (NOTE: for a mechanism use 壞; for a bone use 斷 (duàn, duann)
嫌	xián shyan	V:	think ... (used to express negative feeling), to dislike (something) for a certain negative characteristic
擠 挤	jǐ jii	V: Adj:	to crowd, to squeeze crowded
更別說 更别说	gèng biéshuō genqbyeshuo		don't even mention
向	xiàng shianq	Prep:	to, towards
緊張 紧张	jǐnzhāng jiinjang	Adj:	tight, in short supply
單身 单身	dānshēn danshen	Adj:	single

年紀 年纪	niánjì nianjih	N:	age
輪得到 轮得到	lúnde-dào luen.de-daw	RV:	be able to get (one's) turn
輪 轮	lún luen	N: V:	wheel, e.g., 輪子 to take turns
老劉 老刘	Lǎo Liú Lao Liou		name
老二	Lǎo Èr Lao Ell		the second child
愛人 爱人	àirén ay.ren	N:	spouse
讓 让	ràng ranq	V:	to yield, to give up the right
方便	fāngbiàn fang.biann	Adj:	convenient
嚷	rǎng raang	V:	to yell, to shout out to promote something in an exaggerated manner (in this context)
四個現代化 四个现代化	Sìge Xiàndàihuà Syhg Shianndayhuah	N:	the four modernizations (agriculture, industry, national defense, and science and technology)
現代化 现代化	xiàndàihuà shianndayhuah	V: N:	modernized modernization
化	huà huah		-ize, -ify
老百姓	lǎobǎixìng laobaeshinq	N:	"hundred last names", the common people, civilians
基本	jīběn jibeen	Adj:	basic, fundamental
解決不了	jiějuébu-liǎo jieejyue.bu-leau	RV:	not be able to resolve
解決	jiějué jieejyue	V:	to resolve, to solve

大聲 大声	dàshēng dahsheng	Adv: Adj:	loudly loud
爹	diē die	N:	dad, daddy (local expression, not commonly used)
教師 教师	jiàoshī jiawshy	N:	teacher
黨 党	dǎng daang	N:	(political) party; gang
退休	tuìxiū tueyshiou	V:	to retire
對得起 对得起	duìde-qǐ duey.de-chii	RV:	be able to face (someone)
街道委員 街道委员	jiēdào wěiyuán jie.daw woeiyuan	N:	neighborhood committee
找麻煩 找麻烦	zhǎo-máfán jao-ma.farn	VO:	to cause trouble; to look for trouble
提起	tí-qǐ tyi-chii	RV:	to mention, to bring up
説起 说起	shuō-qǐ shuo-chii	RV:	speaking of ...; to bring up
何必	hébì herbih	Adv:	why must?
留	liú liou	V:	to keep, to stay; remain
小意思	xiǎo yìsī sheau yih.sy	N:	"little intention", not much of anything (polite term referring to gift, said by giver), a token of something
收下	shōuxià shou.shiah	RV:	to take, to accept
文化大革命	Wénhuà Dàgémìng Wenhuah Dahgerminq	N:	The Great Cultural Revolution

自殺 自杀	zìshā tzyhsha	V:	to commit suicide
文革	Wén gě Wen ger	N:	short for 文化大革命
一再	yí-zài i-tzay	Adj:	over and over again
受批鬥 受批斗	shòu pīdòu show pidow	VO:	to be a target of (severe) critcism (political term of Cultural Revolution)
批鬥 批斗	pīdòu pidow	V: N:	to make a public criticism (severe) public criticism
批鬥會 批斗会	pīdòuhuì pidowhuey	N:	meeting for (severe) public criticism
紅衛兵 红卫兵	Hóngwèibīng Horngweybing	N:	the "Red Guards"
打成	dǎ-chéng daa-cherng	RV:	to beat to the point that ...
重傷 重伤	zhòngshāng jonqshang	N:	severe injury 受傷: to be injured
没多久	méi duōjiǔ mei duojeou		before long
上吊	shàngdiào shanqdiaw	V:	to hang oneself

Sentence Patterns

1. 從 ... 開始   starting from; since

⊙ 從大學一年級開始就做了朋友了。
We have been friends since freshman year of college.

(1) 我們從明天開始每天去跑步，好不好？
Starting tomorrow, let's go jogging everyday, OK?

(2) 從現在開始，大家都不准說話。
From now on, nobody is allowed to speak.

(3) 這次的考試我們應該從第三頁開始預備。
For this exam, we should start preparing from page 3.

(4) 你想從哪一課開始學？
From which lesson do you want to start studying?

2. 連 A 都 ... 更別說 B 了   even A is true, not to mention B

⊙ 我們家就這麼一間小破房子，兩個人住都嫌擠，更別說住四個人了。
Our home is just this small deteriorating hut. Even two people living in it is too crowded, not to mention four.

(1) 連碗都洗不好，更別說做飯了。
(He) can't even wash dishes well, not to mention cooking

(2) 在美國連窮人都有汽車，更別說有錢人了。
In the U.S. even poor people have cars, not to mention the rich.

3. 嫌   to dislike; to mind; to complain of; (used to express negative feelings)

⊙ 兩個人住都嫌擠。
Two people living together is already too crowded.

(1) 他總是嫌我開車開得太快。
He always thinks that I'm driving too fast.

(2) 你要是嫌這儿不舒服，就上別的地方去吧。
If you think it's too uncomfortable here, then go to another place.

(3) 我嫌這個東西貴了一點儿。
I think this thing is a bit too expensive.

or 對我來說，這個東西嫌貴了一點儿。
To me, this thing is a bit too expensive

4. 有甚麼好 V 的呢？

What's the worth of ...?   What is the point in ...?   (Rhetorical question)

⊙ 這有甚麼好說的呢？
What's the point of saying this?

(1) 電視有甚麼好看的呢？不是打就是殺。
What does TV have that is worth watching? If it's not violence, then it's murder.

(2) 東西壞了就買個新的吧，有甚麼好生氣的呢？
If the thing is broken, then get a new one. What's the point of getting angry?

5. 何必 ...（呢）？　　　why must ...?　　　(Rhetorical)

⊙ 何必那麼客氣呢？
Why must you be so polite?

(1) 在家裡吃飯也行，何必到飯館去呢？
It's fine eating at home. Why must we go out to a restaurant?

(2) 他不願意跟你去，何必非要他去不可呢？
If he's not willing to go with you why must you make him go?

Excercises

一．完成對話　(Complete the following dialogues with the expressions in parentheses.)

1.　A: 你學中文已經學了兩年了，你看得懂看不懂中文報紙？

　　B: ＿＿＿＿＿＿＿＿＿＿＿＿＿＿＿＿＿＿＿。
　　　　　　　　　　　　　　　　　　　　（連...更別說...）

2.　A: 今天晚上我請客，你想吃什麼？

　　B: ＿＿＿＿＿＿＿＿＿＿＿＿＿＿＿＿＿＿＿

　　　＿＿＿＿＿＿＿＿＿＿＿＿＿＿＿＿＿＿＿。
　　　　　　　　　　　　　　　　　　　（甚麼都...就是...）

3.　A: 中學畢業了，可是找不到工作。找工作真難！

　　B: ＿＿＿＿＿＿＿＿＿＿＿＿＿＿＿＿＿＿＿

　　　＿＿＿＿＿＿＿＿＿＿＿＿＿＿＿＿＿＿＿。
　　　　　　　　　　　　　　　　　　　　　　（別說...）

二．改寫句子　(Rewrite the following sentences according to the words supplied below.)

1.　學了三年中文的人還看不懂中文報紙，學了三個月的中文的人怎麼看得懂呢？

　　＝＿＿＿＿＿＿＿＿＿＿＿＿＿＿＿＿＿＿＿。
　　　　　　　　　　　　　　　　　　　（連...更別說）

2.　文革的時候紅衛兵把他的父親打成了重傷。

　　＝＿＿＿＿＿＿＿＿＿＿＿＿＿＿＿＿＿＿＿。
　　　　　　　　　　　　　　　　　　　　　　（被）

三. 翻譯　　　(Translation)

1.　You have worked for our school your whole life. Now you are going to retire. Please take this (small) gift.

2.　The Chinese government has been promoting the four modernizations since 1980. However, Chinese people are very unhappy because the government still can't solve the basic living problems of the people.

3.　People who want to get married must have the approval of their working unit.

4.　Since they have been assigned different places to work, they hardly see each other.

5.　Can inflation (prices go up) and other fundamental living problems be solved?

6.　How come the price went up again? I don't know anyone who is willing to buy things which are so expensive.

四. 作文　　　(Composition)

在你看來，美國青年有甚麼煩惱？他們的煩惱跟中國青年的煩惱一樣不一樣？

第十三課

中國的人口（一）

Vocabulary

人口	rénkǒu renkoou	N:	population
世界	shìjiè shyhjieh	N:	world
大約　大约	dàyuē dahiue	Adv:	approximately
億　　亿	yì yih	N:	a hundred million
差不多	chàbuduō chah.buduo	Adv:	almost, nearly
佔　　占	zhàn jann	V:	to occupy
全	quán chyuan	Adj:	complete, whole (e.g., 全國, 全家, etc.)
四分之一	sì-fēn zhī-i syh-fen jy-i		one fourth
鄉下　乡下	xiāngxià shiang.shiah	PW:	countryside, rural areas
街	jiē jie	N:	street
口	kǒu koou	M:	measure word for number of people in a family
傳統　传统	chuántǒng chwantoong	N: Adj:	tradition traditional
福氣　福气	fúqì fu.chih	N:	fortune (often referring to family matters) 有福氣: blessed by fortune

115

年老	niánlǎo nianlao	N: old age
保障	bǎozhàng baojanq	V: to secure, to guarantee N: security, guarantee
一向	yíxiàng yishianq	Adv: all along
農業　农业	nóngyè nongyeh	N: "farm profession", agriculture 工業: "labor profession", industry
大量	dàliàng dahlianq	Adj: a great quantity, a large amount
人力	rénlì renlih	N: manpower
地	dì dih	PW: (here) fields (for farming)
保險　保险	bǎoxiǎn baoshean	N: insurance
制度	zhìdù jyhduh	N: system
老年	lǎonián laonian	N: old age
靠	kào kaw	V: "to lean on", to depend on, to rely upon
多子多福	duō zǐ duō fú duo tzyy duo fwu	Many sons (bring) much good fortune.
道理	dàolǐ daw.lii	N: reason 有道理: "have logic", reasonable, rational, meaningful
幾十年來 几十年来	jǐ-shí-nián lái jii-shyr-nian lai	in the past several decades
政治	zhèngzhì jenqjyh	N: politics
各	gè geh	N: various

方面	fāngmiàn fangmiann	M/N:	aspect
改變 改变	gǎibiàn gaebiann	N: V:	change; alteration to change
政府	zhèngfǔ jenqfuu	N:	government
漸漸 渐渐	jiànjiàn jiannx	Adv:	gradually
認識 认识	rènshi renn.shyh	V:	come to understand, realize, recognize
水平	shuǐpíng shoeipyng	N:	level; standard
原因	yuányīn yuan'in	N:	cause
從…起 从…起	cóng ... qǐ tsorng ... chii		from ... (time) on, beginning from ... (to present)
七十年代	qīshí niándài chishyr nianday		1970's
年代	niándài nianday	N:	a decade within a century; period
推行	tuīxíng tueishyng	V:	promote (a policy, a plan), put into action
政策	zhèngcè jenqtseh	N:	policy
提倡	tíchàng tyichanq	V:	to advocate
控制	kòngzhì konqjyh	V:	to control, to keep within limit
增加	zēngjiā tzengjia	N: V:	an increase to increase
對　对	duì duey	Prep:	towards
一定的	yídìng de idinq .de	Adj:	a certain

獎勵 奖励	jiǎnglì jeanglih	N: V:	encouragement to reward; to encourage with a reward
及	jí jyi	Conj:	and (literary)
教育	jiàoyù jiaw.yuh	N: V:	education to educate
安排	ānpái anpair	N: V:	arrangement to arrange
按照	ànzhào annjaw		according to ...
規定 规定	guīdìng gueidinq	N:	stipulation, regulations
而	ér erl	Conj:	but
受…的制裁	shòu ... de zhìcái show ... .de jyhtsair	V:	to be punished by ...
制裁	zhìcái jyhtsair	N: V:	punishment to punish
輿論 舆论	yúlùn yuluenn	N:	public opinion
進入 进入	jìnrù jinnruh	V:	to enter (written)
嚴格 严格	yán'gé yan'ger	Adj:	strict, rigorous (of actions, policies, demands, etc.)
執行 执行	zhíxíng jyrshyng	V:	to implement, to carry out
重男輕女 重男轻女	zhòngnán qīngnǚ jonqnan chingneu		to value boys and think lightly of girls
深	shēn shen	Adj:	profound, deep; (here) deeply rooted
大部份	dàbùfèn dahbuhfenn		the majority, a large part of

農村 农村	nóngcūn nongtsuen	N:	village, rural community
良好	liánghǎo lianghao	Adj:	good (formal)
遇到	yùdào yuh.daw	V:	to encounter; to bump into; to run into
困難 困难	kùn'nán kuenn'nan	N: Adj:	difficulty, hardship difficult
不斷 不断	búduàn buduann	Adv:	unceasingly, continuously
增加	zēngjiā tzengjia	V:	to increase and grow

Sentence Patterns

1. **A 分 之 B**   The fraction B/A

    ⊙ 差不多佔全世界人口的四分之一。
       (It) occupies almost one quarter of the world's population.

    (1) 五分之四
         four-fifths, 4/5

    (2) 二分之一
         one half, 1/2

    (3) 百分之十
         one-tenth, 10%

2. **N1 佔 N2 的 A 分 之 B**   N1 makes up (occupies) B/A of N2

    ⊙ 中國人口佔全世界人口的四分之一。
       The Chinese make up one quarter of the world's population.

    (1) 女學生佔全校學生的三分之一。
         Female students make up one-third of the student body.

    (2) 選中文課的學生佔全校學生的幾分之幾？
         At this school what percentage of students take Chinese (classes)?

3. **不 但 ... 而 且 ...**   not only ... but also ...

    ⊙ 孩子多不但不是福氣而且是一個很重的負擔。
       Not only is having many children not a blessing, but (it's) also a very heavy burden.

    (1) 我不但不喜歡他而且恨他。
         I not only don't like him, I hate him.

(2) 他不但喜歡妳而且要跟妳結婚。

Not only does he like you, but he also wants to marry you.

(3) 這個藥，你吃了不但病不會好而且會更嚴重。

If you take this medicine not only will your (ill) condition not improve, but it will become even more serious.

4. 越 A 越 B　　　the more A the more B

⊙ 孩子越多，越有福氣。

The more children (one has), the more fortunate he is.

(1) 錢越多越好。

The more money (one has) the better.

(2) 窗子越多屋子越亮。

The more windows [it has] the brighter the room.

(3) 他越吃越胖。

The more he eats the fatter he gets.

(4) 這間屋子我越住越不喜歡。

The more I live in this room, the less I like it..

(5) 他跑得越來越快。

He is running faster and faster.

5. 對

⊙ 對只有一個孩子的家庭，政府有一定的獎勵。

To the one-child household the government gives certain encouragements and rewards.

(1) 對這件事我有幾點意見。

I have several opinions about this matter.

(2) 我對歷史很有興趣。

I am very interested in history.

121

(3)　　　多運動對你的身體有好處。
Exercising more is very beneficial to your health.

(4)　　　這件事對我有很大的影響。
This matter greatly influences me.　(This matter has had a great influence on me.)

(5)　　　政府對經濟問題很關心。
The government is very concerned about economic issues.

Excercises

一．完成對話

(Complete the following dialogues with the expressions in parentheses.)

1. A: 中國人為什麼喜歡生男孩？

    B: _____ 。

    （原因）

2. A: 你喜歡不喜歡你的新宿舍？

    B: _____ 。

    （越...越...）

3. A: 中國政府要老百姓多生孩子嗎？

    B: _____ 。

    （不但不...而且）

4. A: 鄉下的地方大，空氣又好，你為什麼住不慣？

    B: _____ 。

    （一向）

二．改寫句子

(Rewrite the following sentences according to the words supplied below.)

1. 有一百個人學中文，在這一百個人裡有五個人去過中國。

    = _____ 。

    （佔）

2. 中國的經濟情形越來越壞跟人口問題有一定的關係。

    = _____ 。

    （使）

3. 看書看得不多，知道的事情就少。

    = _____ 。

    （越...越...）

三. 翻譯　　(Translation)

1. Since China has a serious population problem, the Chinese government should strictly carry out the one-child-per-family policy.

2. If he had two children he would be punished and the second child could not receive a good education.

3. When promoting a policy, the government usually uses a very strict approach (method). If the common people do not carry out the policy according to the government's regulations, they will be punished.

4. People who have received a good education know that the continuous increase in population has had a bad influence on the country's economy.

5. In many countries the people have no freedom of speech, therefore those who oppose the government will usually be punished.

6. When promoting a new policy the government must use education, otherwise it will face many difficulties.

7. Chinese people have many traditional concepts which are already out of date, for example: "the more sons, the more fortunate" "value boys and disregard girls" and "male chauvinism."

四. 作文　　(Composition)

中國的人口政策是什麼？你對這個政策有什麼看法？

第十四課

中國的人口（二）

Vocabulary

人道	réndào rendaw	Adj:	"human-way", humane
完全	wánquán wanchyuan	Adv: Adj:	completely complete
個人 个人	gèrén gehren	N:	each individual
分開 分开	fēnkāi fenkai	RV:	to divide, to separate
譬如	pìrú pihru		for example
州	zhōu jou	N:	state 紐約州: New York state
綁 绑	bǎng baang	V:	to tie (shoes, etc.) 綁安全帶: to fasten a seat belt
罰 罚	fá far	VO:	to penalize, to punish 罰錢: to fine (an amount of money)
照顧 照顾	zhàogù jawguh	V:	to take care of
想像 想象	xiǎngxiàng sheangshianq	V:	to imagine
造成	zàochéng tzawcherng	RV:	to create (a certain situation, usually negative)
末期	mòqī mohchi	TW:	last part of (a period of time)
鬧饑荒 闹饥荒	nào-jīhuāng naw-jihuang	VO:	to be plagued by famine

千千萬萬 千千万万	qiānqiānwànwàn chianxwannx		"thousands and ten-thousands", very many
錯誤 错误	cuòwù tsuoh.wuh	N:	mistake
過多 过多	guòduō guohduo	Adj:	too much, excessive
與其…不如 与其…不如	yǔqí A bùrú B yeuchyi A buru B		doing A is not as good as doing B
反而	fǎnér faanerl	Adv:	on the contrary
些	xiē shie		somewhat (more or less)
發達 发达	fādá fadar	V: Adj:	to develop, advance developed; advanced
條件 条件	tiáojiàn tyaujiann	N:	conditions; qualifications; criteria
台灣 台湾	Táiwān Tair'uan	PW:	Taiwan
香港	Xiānggǎng Shianggaang	PW:	Hong Kong
密度	mìdù mihduh	N:	density
缺點 缺点	quēdiǎn chiuedean	N:	shortcomings, flaws
變成 变成	biànchéng bianncherng	V:	to become
股	gǔ guu	M:	a bunch of, a blast of
力量	lìliang lihlianq	N:	strength, power
獨生子女 独生子女	dúshēng zǐnǚ dwusheng tzyyneu	N:	only child 獨生子: only son 獨生女: only daughter

慣壞 慣坏	guàn-huài guann-huay	RV:	to spoil
祖父母	zǔfùmǔ tzuufuhmuu	N:	grandparents (paternal) 祖父: grandfather (paternal) 祖母: grandmother (paternal) 外祖父: grandfather (maternal) 外祖母: grandmother (maternal)
注意力	zhùyìlì juhyihlih	N:	attention
集中	jízhōng jyijong	V:	to concentrate (on)
由於 由于	yóuyú youyu		due to, as a result of
過份 过分	guòfèn guohfenn	Adv: Adj:	too much; excessively excessive
保護 保护	bǎohù baohuh	V: N:	to protect protection
往往	wǎngwǎng woangx	Adv:	often, usually
變 变	biàn biann	V:	to change, undergo a change
自私	zìsī tzyhsy	Adj:	selfish
確實 确实	quèshí chiuehshyr	Adv:	really, truly
制定	zhìdìng jyhdinq	V:	to stipulate, to establish (law)

Sentence Patterns

1. 一方面 ...（另）一方面 ...

on one hand..., on the other hand ...

⊙ 這一方面是因為政策上的錯誤；另一方面，人口過多也是造成大饑荒的主要原因。

On the one hand this (the great famine) is due to mistakes in the policy, on the other hand the extremely large population is also a major cause of the great famine.

(1) A: 你為甚麼來申請這個工作？
A: Why are you applying for this job?

B: 一方面是因為我很喜歡旅行；另一方面我對導遊的工作很有興趣所以我來申請這個工作。
B: On the one hand because I like to travel, on the other hand because I am interested in being a tour guide. That's why I am applying for this job.

(2) 他一方面跟我說他同意我的看法，一方面又在別人面前批評我。
On the one hand he told me that he agrees with my view, on the other hand he criticized me in front of others.

(3) 我一方面覺得很高興，一方面覺得很難過。
On the one hand I feel very happy, on the other hand, I feel very sad.

(4) 買東西的時候一方面要注意價錢，一方面要看看東西好不好。
When purchasing things, one must take notice of the prices while looking to see if the product is good.

(5) 老師應該一方面教書，一方面做研究。
The teacher should teach while doing research.

2. 與其 A 不如 B   A is not as good as B

⊙ 我想與其讓孩子生下來，然後餓死，不如不生。
I feel that it's better not to have children at all than to have children and then afterwards starve them to death.

(1) 你與其出去看電影不如去看書。
It's better for you to read than to see a movie.

(2) 與其學物理不如學電子計算機。
Studying physics is not as good as studying computers.

3. 反而   on the contrary

⊙ 這樣反而人道些。
This way on the contrary is more humane.

(1) 漂亮的衣服很便宜，難看的衣服反而很貴。
The pretty clothes are inexpensive; the ugly clothes, on the contrary, are expensive.

(2) 好的書沒有人看，壞的書反而看的人很多。
Nobody reads good books; however, everyone reads the bad ones.

(3) 他的病不但沒好，反而更厲害了。
His sickness not only did not get better, on the contrary it got even worse.

(4) 他不但沒謝我，反而罵了我一頓。
Not only did he not thank me, but he even gave me a scolding.

4. （所以）A 是因為 B（的關係／緣故）   A is due to B

⊙ 中國人把經濟不發達...說成是因為人口太多的關係。
The Chinese say that the undeveloped economy is caused by the excessively large population.

(1) 他（所以）沒來上課是因為他生病了（的關係／緣故）。
  = 因為生病了所以他沒來上課。

129

The reason he didn't come to class was that he was sick.

(2)　你 的 功課 (所以) 不好 是不是 因為 不夠 用功 的 關係？

Is it because you don't work hard enough that your homework is not good?

5. 不是 … 而是 …　　It's not A, but rather B

⊙　我看中國的人口政策真正的問題不在現在而是在將來。

I think that the real problems of China's population policy are not apparent now but will appear in the future.

(1)　重男輕女不是一個現代的觀念而是一個傳統的觀念。

Favoring boys and disfavoring girls is not a modern concept, but is rather a traditional concept.

(2)　中國不是資本主義的國家而是社會主義的國家。

China is not a capitalist country but rather a socialist country.

6. 由於　　due to (written or formal use)

⊙　由於過分地保護，孩子往往變得不能獨立而且自私。

Due to overprotection, the child often becomes incapable of living independently and becomes selfish.

(1)　由於經濟不發達所以人民的生活水平很低。

Due to the undeveloped economy the people's standard of living is very low.

(2)　很多人不敢多生孩子是由於怕政府制裁。

Many people don't dare to have more children due to fear of governmental punishment.

7. 所   emphatic adverb similar to "that" or "which" in English (optional use)

⊙   有些問題確實是制定政策的時候所沒有想到的。

There are a few problems that were evidently not considered at the time of establishing the policy.

(1)   我所看的書都是跟歷史有關係的。

The books I read are all related to history.

(2)   書上所說的我都懂了。

I understand everything in the book.

(3)   照老師所說的，中國文化跟美國文化有很大的不同。

According to what the teacher said, there is a big difference between Chinese culture and American culture.

Excercises

一． 完成對話　　(Complete the following dialogues with the expression in parentheses.)

1.　A: 你覺得孩子多是福氣嗎？

　　B: _____。
　　　　　　　　　　　　　　　　　　　　（不是...而是...）

2.　A: 我想畢業以後到香港去學中文。

　　B: _____。
　　　　　　　　　　　　　　　　　　　　　　（與其）

3.　A: 你昨天為什麼沒來上課？

　　B: _____。
　　　　　　　　　　　　　　　　（一方面...一方面...）

4.　A: 昨天你考得好不好？

　　B: 真奇怪，難的課我考得很好_____

　　　_____。
　　　　　　　　　　　　　　　　　　　　　　（反而）

5.　A: 他一向喜歡經濟，不喜歡歷史。今年他一定又選了經濟
　　　課。

　　B: 不對，_____。
　　　　　　　　　　　　　　　　　（不但不/沒...反而）

二． 改寫句子　　(Rewrite the following sentences according to the words supplied below.)

1.　我喜歡看經濟方面的書。

　　=_____。
　　　　　　　　　　　　　　　　　　　　　　（所）

132

2. 由於經濟不發達，人民的生活水平很低。

= _____ 。

(...所以...是因為...)

= _____ 。

(A是因為B的緣故)

3. 因為開車開得太快，警察罰了我一百塊錢。

= _____ 。

(被)

三.　　翻譯　　(Translation)

1. The "one child per family policy" has many flaws. The child can become selfish and too dependent on his parents.

2. The new agriculture policy that the government recently laid out did not make the economic situation better, on the contrary, it caused a big famine.

3. You have been spoiled by your parents. You are 30 years old. How can you still ask your mother to clean your room?

4. Parents have the obligation to take care of and protect their children. If a child dies because he did not fasten his seatbelt, his parents will be punished by the government.

5. From my point of view, having children is a person's basic right. It has nothing to do with the government. It is very inhumane for the government to control the population by way of abortion.

6. Although he is the only child in the family, he is not spoiled by his parents. They don't give him all their attention. They want him to be independent and able to take care of himself.

7. Hong Kong is a place with a big population. But the economy there is well-developed and the standard of living is very high. Therefore I think that a big population is not necessarily a shortcoming but sometimes can be a strength.

8. I think it's inevitable that an only child will be spoiled by his parents, and will grow up to be not only not independent, but also selfish.

9. Abortion is very dangerous, therefore it is better to teach women about contraception than to make them have abortions.

四．作文　　　(Composition)

請你說一說你對中國的人口問題的看法。

第十五課

北京．上海．台北

Vocabulary

好久不見 好久不见	hǎojiǔbújiàn haojeoubujiann		"long time no see" 好久: a long time
亞洲　亚洲	Yàzhōu Yahjou	PW:	Asia
日本	Rìběn Ryhbeen	PW:	Japan
泰國　泰国	Tàiguó Taygwo	PW:	Thailand
韓國　韩国	Hánguó Harngwo	PW:	Korea
怪不得	guàibu-dé guay.bu-der	Adv:	no wonder
假期	jiàqī jiahchi	N:	vacation
論文　论文	lùnwén luennwen	N:	thesis, dissertation
實驗室　实验室	shíyànshì shyryannshyh	N:	laboratory (for scientific experiments)
用功	yòng-gōng yonq-gong	Adj:	(study) diligently
難說　难说	nánshuō nanshuo		hard to say, hard to tell
印象	yìnxiàng yinnshianq	N:	impression
有趣	yǒuqù yeouchiuh	Adj:	interesting

135

現象　现象	xiànxiàng shiannshianq	N:	phenomenon
習慣　习惯	xíguàn shyiguann	V: N:	to be accustomed to habit, what (one) is accustomed to
一般說來 一般说来	yì-bān shuō-lái i-ban shuo-lai		generally speaking
抽水馬桶 抽水马捅	chōushuǐ mǎtǒng choushoei maatoong	N:	"pump water horse bucket", toilet
蹲	dūn duen	V:	to squat
用不慣　用不惯	yòngbú-guàn yonq.bu-guann	RV:	cannot get used to using
衛生　卫生	wèishēng weysheng	Adj: N:	"protect life", sanitary sanitation
除非	chúfēi chwufei	Adv:	unless
設備　设备	shèbèi shehbey	N:	facilities
住家	zhùjiā juhjia	N:	residence
公共	gōnggòng gonggonq	Adj:	public
澡堂	zǎotáng tzaotarng	N:	bathhouse
走路	zǒu-lù tzoou-luh	VO:	to walk
交通	jiāotōng jiautong	N:	traffic; transportation (systems)
情況　情况	qíngkuàng chyngkuanq	N:	condition
好像…似的 好象…似的	hǎoxiàng ... shìde haoshianq ... shyh.de		it seems that ...

怕	pà pah	Adj:	to be afraid of, fear
計程車　计程车	jìchéngchē jihcherngche	N:	"measure distance vehicle", taxicab
橫衝直撞 横冲直撞	héngchōngzhí zhuàng herngchongjyr juanq		"to charge vertically and horizontally", to drive recklessly
好像⋯的樣子 好象⋯的样子	hǎoxiàng ... .de yàngzi haoshianq ... .de yanqtz		it seems like; like
規則　规则	guīzé gueitzer	N:	rules, regulations (traffic)
紅綠燈　红绿灯	hónglǜdēng horngliuhdeng	N:	traffic light
斑馬線　斑马线	bānmǎxiàn banmaashiann	N:	"zebra line", pedestrian crosswalk
看	kān kan	V:	keep an eye on
發生不了作用 发生不了作用	fāshēngbù-liǎo zuòyòng fasheng.bu-leau tzuohyonq	RV:	cannot be effective
作用	zuòyòng tzuohyonq	N:	effect; function, usefulness
停	tíng tyng	V:	to stop
照你這麼説來 照你这么说来	zhào nǐ zenme shuō-lái ... jaw .nii tzemm shuo-lai ...		according to what you are saying ...
千萬　千万	qiānwàn chianwann	Adv:	by all means
誤會　误会	wùhuì wuh.huey	V: N:	to misunderstand misunderstanding

特色	tèsè tehseh	N:	characteristic (often used in a positive sense)
首都	shǒudū shooudu	N:	"head city", (nation's) capital
所在地	suǒzàidì suootzaydih	N:	location
中心	zhōngxīn jongshin	N:	center
古老	gǔlǎo guulao	Adj:	ancient
之一	zhī-yī jy-i		one of the ...
明朝	Míngcháo Mingchaur	TW:	Ming dynasty (1368 - 1644)
清朝	Qīngcháo Chingchaur	TW:	Ch'ing dynasty (1644 - 1911)
建築　建筑	jiànzhù jiannjuh	N:	building, architectural construction
參觀　参观	cānguān tsanguan	V:	to visit (an organization, a famous site, etc.)
貿易　贸易	màoyì maw.yih	N:	trade
市中心	shì zhōngxīn shyh jongshin	PW:	center of town, downtown
歐洲　欧洲	Ōuzhōu Oujou	PW:	Europe
風味儿　风味儿	fēngwèr fengwell	N:	style, flavor (abstract)
世紀　世纪	shìjì shyhjih	TW:	century
末年	mònián mohnian	TW:	the last years (of a century of dynasty)
初年	chūnián chunian	TW:	the beginning of a period of years

侵略	qīnlüè chinliueh	V: N:	to invade invasion
西化	xīhuà shihuah	Adj:	Westernized
吸引	xīyǐn shiyiin	V:	attract
成千上萬 成千上万	chéngqiān shàngwàn cherngqian shanqwann		"reach thousand upon ten thousand", very many
觀光客 观光客	guān'guāngkè guan'guangkeh	N:	tourists
從前 从前	cóngqián tsorngchyan	TW:	in the past, before
開放 开放	kāifàng kaifanq	Adj: V:	unrestricted, open to open
據…説 据…说	jù … shuō jiuh … shuo		according to …
生產 生产	shēngchǎn shengchaan	N: V:	production to produce
倍	bèi bey		times (as in: five times as big)
農民 农民	nóngmín nongmin	N:	peasant
收入	shōurù shouruh	N:	income
提高	tígāo tyigau	V:	to raise
改善 改善	gǎishàn gaeshann	V:	to refine, to improve
缺貨 缺货	quē-huò chiue-huoh	VO:	"short of goods", to be out of stock, to be sold out
物價 物价	wùjià wuhjiah	N:	commodity prices

治安	zhì'ān jyh'an	N:	public security
方式	fāngshì fangshyh	N:	style (of), mode
大致	dàzhì dahjyh	Adv:	approximately, generally, in broad terms
髮型 发型	fàxíng fahshyng	N:	hair style
服裝 服装	fúzhuāng fwujuang	N:	clothing (formal)
小説 小说	xiǎoshuō sheaushuo	N:	novel, fictitional writings
選擇 选择	xuǎnzé sheuantzer	N: V:	a selection to select
誘惑 诱惑	yòuhuò yowhuoh	N: V:	temptation to tempt, to lure
因此	yīncǐ intsyy	Conj:	therefore (formal)
搶劫 抢劫	qiǎngjié cheangjye	N:	robbery (formal)
案子	ànzi anntz	N:	(court) case
比較 比较	bǐjiào biijiaw		to compare
資本主義 资本主义	zīběn zhǔyì tzybeen juuyih	N:	capitalism
道路	dàolù dawluh	N:	route, road
共産主義 共产主义	gòngchǎn zhǔyì gonqchaan juuyih	N:	communism
言論自由 言论自由	yánlùn zìyóu yanluenn tzyhyou	N:	freedom of speech

在…內	zài ... nèi tzay ... ney		within ...
範圍　范围	fànwéi fannwei	N:	scope, range
批評　批评	pīpíng pipyng	V: N:	to criticize criticism
提出	tíchū tyichu	V:	to raise, to bring up
與　　与	yǔ yeu	Conj:	and (written)
絕對　绝对	juéduì jyueduey	Adv:	absolutely; definitely
允許　允许	yǔnxǔ yeunsheu	V: N:	to allow, to permit permission

Sentence Patterns

1. 原來   originally; formerly; it turned out to be

    ⊙   原來你去了亞洲，怪不得幾個月都沒看到你。
        So it turns out you've been in Asia; no wonder I haven't seen you for a few
        months.

        原來 . . . （怪不得）

        (1)   原來你到外國去旅行了，怪不得我找不到你。
              So you went travelling abroad, no wonder I couldn't find you.

        (2)   你的中文說得這麼好，原來是因為你在中國住了
              一年。
              No wonder your Chinese is so good; you lived in China for a year.

        (3)   我的筆找來找去都找不到，原來是他拿走了。
              No wonder I couldn't find my pen anywhere; he took it.

        原來 . . . 現在 ／ 後來

        (4)   我原來是學文學的，現在學物理了。
              I was originally a literature student, (but) now I'm studying physics.

        (5)   他原來住在美國西部，後來到東部來念書了。
              He originally lived in the western part of the United States then later
              came East to study.

        (6)   這輛車原來是我的，後來我賣給他了。
              This car originally belonged to me, then I later sold it to him.

2. **Time Duration**

    ⊙   幾個月都沒看到你。
        I haven't seen you for a few months.

        Verb + Time Duration

(1) 他要在這儿住兩個禮拜。
He wants to live here for two weeks.

(2) 他只學了一年中文。
He studied only one year of Chinese.

(3) 這本書我看了三天。
I read the book for three days.

Time Duration + Negative Verb

(4) 要是我三天不吃飯一定會餓死。
If I don't eat for three days I will definitely starve to death.

(5) 我有一個月沒給母親打電話了。
I haven't called my mother in a month.

(6) 我好幾天都沒看報所以甚麼新聞都不知道。
I haven't read newspapers for several days, so I don't know of any news.

3. A 對 B 的 印 象 SV
   = A 對 B 有 SV 的 印 象
   = B 給 A 留 下 了 SV 的 印 象

⊙ 我對中國跟台灣的印象最深。
I have the deepest impression of China and Taiwan.

(1) 這幾個城市給我留下了很深的印象。
These several cities have left me with a very deep impression.

(2) 我對這幾個城市有很深的印象。
I have very deep impressions of these several cities.

(3) 我對這幾個城市的印象很深。
The impression I have of these several cities is very deep.

143

4. 除非   unless

⊙ 除非是大旅館或設備比較好的房子，一般住家是沒有洗澡設備的。
Unless it's a big hotel or a rather well-equipped house, most households do not have shower facilities.

(1) 除非是結了婚而且有孩子的人，別的人都是申請不到房子的。
= 別的人是申請不到房子的，除非是結了婚而且有孩子的人才申請得到房子。
Unless one is married and has children, he cannot apply for a house.

(2) 除非自己有廚房，每個人都得在學校的餐廳吃飯。
= 每個人都得在學校的餐廳吃飯，除非自己有廚房才可以不在學校的餐廳吃飯。
Unless a person has a kitchen, everyone must eat in the school cafeteria.

(3) 在中國，一般的老百姓是買不起汽車的，除非是非常有錢的人。
= 除非是非常有錢的人才買得起汽車。
In China, most people can't afford to buy cars unless they are very rich.

(4) 除非天氣好，我是不出去的。
Unless the weather is good, I'm not going out.

5. 好像...（似的）   to seem; to be like

⊙ 在台北開車的人都好像不怕死似的。
In Taipei, all the drivers seems unafraid of death.

(1) 他好像沒聽見我說話似的。
He seems to have not heard me speak.

(2) 你好像對北京很熟悉。
You seem to be very familiar with Beijing.

144

6. **千萬**   imperative intensifier -- "by all means"; "must"

⊙ 你可千萬別誤會我的意思。
By all means don't misunderstand me.

千萬得

(1) 明天你千萬得來幫我的忙。
Tomorrow you must come and help me.

(2) 你千萬得小心開車。
Do drive carefully.

(3) 你千萬得注意安全。
Be sure to pay attention to safety.

千萬別

(4) 你千萬別在深夜的時候在外頭走路。
By all means don't walk outside late at night.

(5) 你千萬別相信他的話。
You must under no circumstances believe what he says.

(6) 回家的時候千萬別忘了買報紙。
When you go home, by all means don't forget to buy the newspaper.

7. **A 是 B 的 所 在 地**   A is the site of B

⊙ 北京是中國首都的所在地。
Peking is the site of China's capital.

(1) 紐約是聯合國的所在地。
New York is where the United Nations is located.

(2) 華盛頓D.C.是美國首都的所在地。
The capital of the United States is located in Washington D.C.

8. 之一　　　one of the

⊙　北京是中國最古老的城市之一。
Beijing is one of China's oldest cities.

(1)　中國是世界上人口最多的國家之一。
China is one of the most populous nations in the world.

(2)　這門課是我最喜歡的課之一。
This course is one of my favorite courses.

(3)　這所大學是美國最小的大學之一。
This university is one of the smallest universities in the United States.

(4)　這是我到這所大學念書的原因之一。
This is one of the reasons I came to this college.

9. A 跟 B 像　　　to be alike; to resemble

⊙　這個大城市跟香港很像。
This big city is similar to Hong Kong.

(1)　他跟他母親很像。
He and his mother are very much alike.

(2)　你寫的字跟我寫的字一點儿都不像。
Your written characters and mine are not the least bit similar.

(3)　中國人的樣子跟日本人的樣子像不像？
Is the (physical) appearance of the Chinese people very similar to that of the Japanese people?

10. 拿 A 跟 B 比較　　　When comparing A and B

⊙　拿中國跟美國比較，中國還是一個相當安全的地方。
When comparing China with the United States, China is a rather safe place.

(1)　拿實驗課跟歷史課比較，歷史課有趣得多。

146

When comparing the lab course with the history course the history course is much more interesting.

(2)　拿高中跟大學比較，大學的學生有比較多的自由。

When comparing high school with college, college students have more freedom.

(3)　拿台北跟香港比較，這兩個城市有許多相同的地方。

When comparing Taipei to Hong Kong, these two cities have many similarities.

Excercises

一．完成對話　(Complete the following dialogues with the expressions in parentheses.)

1. A: 為甚麼你不想住在紐約？

   B: _____。
   　　　　　　　　　　　　　　　　　　　　　(印象)

2. A: 為甚麼沒有人願意跟他住一間屋子？

   B: _____。
   　　　　　　　　　　　　　　　　　　　　　(印象)

3. A: 你明天會不會去參加晚會？

   B: _____。
   　　　　　　　　　　　　　　　　　　　　　(除非)

4. A: 在中國每個人家裡都有抽水馬桶嗎？

   B: 不對，不對，_____。
   　　　　　　　　　　　　　　　　　　　　(除非...才...)

5. A: 上海有甚麼特色？

   B: _____。
   　　　　　　　　　　　　　　　　　　　　　(之一)

6. A: 為甚麼北京是一個要緊的地方？

   B: _____。
   　　　　　　　　　　　　　　　　　　　　　(所在地)

7. A: 住在城市跟住在鄉下有甚麼不同？

   B: _____。
   　　　　　　　　　　　　　　　　　　　　　(比較)

8. A: 紐約的車子真多啊！

   B: _____。
   　　　　　　　　　　　　　　　　　　　　　(怪不得)

9. A: 奇怪，他今天怎麼沒來上課？

   B: 他上紐約去看大夫了。

148

A: _____ 。

(原來...怪不得...)

二．改寫句子   (Rewrite the following sentences according to the words supplied below.)

1. 與其到台灣去旅行不如到香港去旅行。

    = _____ 。

    (拿A跟B比較)

2. 沒看過這本書的人都不知道這本書的作者是誰。

    = _____ 。

    (除非...才...)

三．翻譯   (Translation)

1. Big cities have many problems, along with the high density population and chaotic traffic, their public security is also bad.

2. People usually are not familiar with Chinese history unless they major in East Asian Studies.

3. Taipei is the economic center of Taiwan and possibly the most modernized city in the whole country. It attracts thousands of (very many) tourists every year.

4. Beijing is the location of the nation's capital. The buildings in Beijing leave very deep impressions on people; however, daily life there is not very convenient.

5. Taiwan is one of the places with the worst traffic in the whole world. It seems that taxi drivers don't understand the traffic regulations.. Usually, traffic lights and pedestrian crosswalks don't have the proper effect.

6. Since he had taken a trip to Asia, I didn't see him for almost a month.

7. This summer, in order to write my graduation thesis, I didn't go anywhere. Most of the time I stayed in the library.

8. It is very dangerous to drive in this city. As the drivers usually don't obey the traffic rules, the traffic lights can't function effectively unless there are policemen standing beside them.

9. Since the economic policy is more open than before, the production of the village has increased many times. The income of the peasants has also risen.

10. Beijing is one of the oldest cities in China. Every year thousands of tourists go there to visit.

11. Beijing is China's capital, it is also the political and cultural center of China.

12. Every year there are many tourists visiting the World Trade Center.

13. Due to the fact that the economic policy has opened up, the Chinese people's lives have improved.

14. Freedom of speech means that the general public has the freedom to criticize the government and the ability to raise opinions which are different from that of the government.

15. As far as culture and language are concerned, Japan was greatly influenced by China during the T'ang Dynasty.

四．作文　　　(Composition)

1. 請你介紹一個城市。(城市的名字可以用英文)

2. 從這學期學過的課文請你談一談現在你覺得中國是一個
甚麼樣的國家；換一句話說，你對中國有甚麼印象。

第十六課

孔子

Vocabulary

孔子	Kǒngzǐ Koongtzyy		Confucius (551 - 479 B.C.)
偉大 伟大	wěidà woeidah	Adj:	great (of a person and abstract entities, in terms of significance, not for excitement)
思想家	sīxiǎngjiā sysheangjia	N:	thinker, philosopher
教育家	jiàoyùjiā jiawyuhjia	N:	educator (distinguished and well-known)
儒家學説	Rújiā xuéshuō Rujia shyueshuo	N:	Confucianism
儒家	Rújiā Rujia	N:	Confucian School
學説 学说	xuéshuō shyueshuo	N:	theory, doctrine
創始人 创始人	chuàngshǐrén chuanqshyyren	N:	founder
西元	xīyuán shiyuan	TW:	A.D. 西元前：B.C.
春秋時代 春秋时代	Chūnqiū shídài Chuenchiou shyrday	TW:	Spring and Autumn Period (722 - 484 B.C.)
分裂	fēnliè fenlieh	V:	broken up (of a country)
統一 统一	tǒngyī toong'i	Adj:	unified (of a country)
魯國 鲁国	Lǔguó Luugwo	N:	the state of Lu

151

山東　山东	Shāndōng Shandong	PW:	Shandong Province
個子　个子	gèzi gehtz	N:	size (of a person); height (of a person)
高個ㄦ　高个ㄦ	gāogèr gaugell	N:	a tall person
窮　穷	qióng chyong	Adj:	poor
成人	chéngrén cherngren	V:	to become an adult
做官	zuòguān tzuoguan		to be an official
滿意　满意	mǎnyì maanyih	Adj:	satisfied with
離開　离开	líkāi likai	V:	to leave
鄰近　邻近	línjìn linjinn	Adj:	nearby
旅行	lǚxíng leushyng	V:	to travel
同時　同时	tóngshí torngshyr		at the same time; simultaneously
一生	yì-shēng i-sheng	N:	throughout one's life, one's whole life
願望　愿望	yuànwàng yuannwanq	N:	dream, hope, wish
通過　通过	tōngguò tongguoh		by means of, through
君主	jūnzhǔ jiunjuu	N:	ruler
實現　实现	shíxiàn shyrshiann	V:	to realize (ideal, dream, hope, etc.)
理想	lǐxiǎng liisheang	N:	ideal

賞識 賞识	shǎngshì (shí) shaangshyh	V:	to appreciate (an inferior)
才能	cáinéng tsairneng	N:	ability, talent
最後 最后	zuìhòu tzueyhow	TW:	in the end
失望	shīwàng shywanq	Adj:	"lose hope", to be dissapointed
家鄉 家乡	jiāxiāng jiashiang	N:	home, area in which one was born or grew up
公元	gōngyuán gongyuan		A.D.
機會 机会	jīhuì jihuey	N:	opportunity
卻 却	què chiueh	Conj:	but (written)
主流	zhǔliú juuliou	N:	main current
朝代	cháodài chaurday	N:	dynasty
傳説 传说	chuánshuō chwanshuo		according to tradition
論語 论语	Lúnyǔ Luenyeu	N:	*The Analects*
凡是	fánshì farnshyh		whoever ...; whatever ...
受教育	shòu-jiàoyù show-jiawyuh	VO:	to receive education, to be educated
注意	zhùyì juhyih	V: N:	to pay attention to attention
孝順 孝顺	xiàoshùn shiawshuenn	VO: Adj:	to show filial devotion to one's parents to be filial (to parents)
耶穌 耶稣	Yēsū Iesu		Jesus

敵人 敌人	dírén dyiren	N: enemy
左臉 左脸	zuǒliǎn tzoolean	N: left cheek
轉 转	zhuǎn joan	V: to turn
恨	hèn henn	V: to hate
特別	tèbié tehbye	Adv: especially Adj: special
實際 实际	shíjì shyrjih	Adj: realistic, practical
做不到	zuòbú-dào tzuoh.bu-daw	RV: cannot be accomplished
教訓 教训	jiàoxùn jiawshiunn	N: a teaching, a lesson
舊 旧	jiù jiow	Adj: old
秩序	zhìxù jyhshiuh	N: order, sequence here: social order
有權 有权	yǒuquán yeou chyuan	Adj: powerful, authoritative
有勢 有势	yǒu shì yeou shyh	Adj: powerful
有利	yǒu lì yeou lih	Adj: advantageous
有學問 有学问	yǒu xuéwèn yeou shyuewenn	Adj: learned, erudite
學者 学者	xuézhě shyuejee	N: scholar
古代	gǔdài guuday	TW: ancient era or period
經典 经典	jīngdiǎn jingdean	N: (Chinese) classics

整理	zhěnglǐ jeeng.lii	V:	to put in order, to organize
活動 活动	huódòng hwodonq	N:	activities
以及	yǐjí yiijyi	Conj:	as well as; and (literary)
當時 当时	dāngshí dangshyr	TW:	at that time
漢朝 汉朝	Hàncháo Hannchaur	TW:	Han dynasty (206 B.C. - 220 A.D.)
學術思想 学术思想	xuéshù sīxiǎng shyueshuh sysheang	N:	academic philosophy
代表	dàibiǎo daybeau	N: V:	representative to represent

Sentence Patterns

1.　只好　　　to have to; the only alternative is ...

⊙　因為孔子不滿意魯國的政治，只好離開魯國。
Because Confucius was unsatisfied with the politics of the Lu State, he had no choice but to leave the Lu State.

(1)　我本來想上中國去旅行，後來因為沒有錢只好不去了。
Originally I wanted to travel to China. Later, because I had no money, I had no choice but not to go.

(2)　他不喜歡這間屋子，可是因為沒有別的屋子，他只好住了。
He doesn't like this room, but because there were no other rooms he had no choice but to live here.

2.　凡是　　　all those (that) ...

⊙　凡是受過教育的中國人差不多都讀過這本書。
Almost all educated Chinese have read this book.

(1)　凡是學過中文的人，都知道中文的語法並不難。
Anyone who has learned Chinese knows that Chinese grammar is actually not difficult.

(2)　凡是去過紐約的人都知道那儿的交通很亂。
Anyone who has been to New York knows that the traffic there is chaotic.

3. **A 對 B 有利**   A is advantageous to B; A benefits B

⊙   這對有權有勢的人往往是有利的。
This is often advantageous to those with power and influence.

(1)   這個計劃對我沒有利。
This plan does not benefit me.

(2)   上這門課對將來找工作有沒有利？
Will taking this course be beneficial to my job search?

Excercises

一．完成對話　　(Complete the following dialogues with the expressions in parentheses.)

1.　A: 為什麼中國人覺得孔子是一個偉大的人？

　　B: _____ 。
　　　　　　　　　　　　　　　　　　　　　　　　（由於）

2.　A: 所有學中文的學生都得聽錄音帶？

　　B: 對了，_____ 。
　　　　　　　　　　　　　　　　　　　　　　　　（凡是）

3.　A: 下個學期你有甚麼計劃？

　　B: _____ 。
　　　　　　　　　　　　　　　　　　　　　　　　（同時）

4.　A: 你喜歡不喜歡這本教材？

　　B: _____ 。
　　　　　　　　　　　　　　　　　　　　　　　　（滿意）

二．翻譯　　　　(Translation)

1.　If you were realistic, you wouldn't have asked me to love my enemy.

2.　He is not satisfied with the situation in which the political system is advantageous to powerful people in this country.

3.　My biggest wish in life is to become a great educator. I hope that this wish will be realized one day.

4.　While he was alive, he was a very learned scholar; he read almost all the books concerning Confucianism.

5.　The reason he could not find a job was not because no one could appreciate his ability but rather that his grades were not good enough.

6.　I'm not satisfied with the American educational system. Due to the fact that teachers are poorly compensated, many capable and learned people are not willing to teach.

三．作文　　　(Composition)

1. 如果你是教中文的老師，你會不會教《孔子》這一課？為甚麼？

2. 請你討論“愛你的敵人”這個觀念。

第十七課

長 城 與 運 河

Vocabulary

長城 长城	chángchéng charngcherng	N:	The Great Wall
運河 运河	yùnhé yunnher	N:	the Grand Canal, canal
工程	gōngchéng gongcherng	N:	construction; engineering
萬里長城 万里长城	Wànlǐ Chángchéng Wannlii Charngcherng		"ten thousand-mile long wall", The Great Wall
全長 全长	quáncháng chyuancharng	N:	entire length
公里	gōnglǐ gonglii		kilometer
照	zhào jaw	V:	according to
一般	yì-bān i-ban	Adj:	general; ordinary
說法 说法	shuōfǎ shuofaa	N:	way of saying
秦始皇	Qín Shǐhuáng Chyn Shyyhwang		The First Emperor of the Ch'in dynasty
建	jiàn jiann	V:	to construct, to build
大多	dàduō dahduo	Adv:	mostly, for the most part
明代	míngdài mingday	TW:	Ming Dynasty (1368 - 1644)

修築 修筑	xiūzhù shioujuh	V:	to build, to constuct
防止	fángzhǐ farngjyy	V:	to guard against, to prevent
北方	běifāng beeifang	PW:	northern part; the North
南邊 南边	nánbiān nanbian	PW:	south
到底	dàodǐ dawdii	Adv:	in actuality, after all
起作用	qǐzuòyòng chiitzuohyonq	VO:	to show effect
逃	táo taur	V:	to escape
外患	wàihuàn wayhuann	N:	foreign trouble
宋朝	Sòngcháo Sonqchaur	TW:	Song Dynasty (960 - 1279)
整個 整个	zhěng-gè jeeng-geh	Adj:	the whole
亡	wáng wang	V:	perish (e.g., dynasty, country, etc.)
蒙古人	Měnggǔrén Mengguuren	N:	a Mongolian
認爲 认为	rènwéi rennwei	V:	to think, to have the opinion that ..., to consider (something to be true)
國防 国防	guófáng gwofarng	N:	national defense
軍事 军事	jūnshì jiunshyh	N:	military affairs
意義 意义	yìyì yihyih	N:	significance
極小 极小	jíxiǎo jyisheau	Adj:	extremely small

往	wàng wanq	Prep:	toward
發展 发展	fāzhǎn fajaan	N: V:	development to develop
以北	yǐběi yiibeei		(to the) north of ...
以南	yǐnán yiinan		(to the) south of ...
落後 落后	luòhòu luohhow	Adj:	underdeveloped; (has fallen) behind
地理	dìlǐ dihlii	N:	geography
緣故 缘故	yuángù yuanguh	N:	reason
流血流汗	liúxiě liúhàn lioushiee liouhann		"bleeding and sweating", with great suffering
大運河 大运河	dà yùnhé dah yunnher		The Grand Canal
人工	réngōng rengong	Adj:	manpower; man-made; artificial
開建 开建	kāijiàn kaijiann	V:	to open up and build
河流	héliú herliou	N:	rivers, formal
杭州	Hángzhōu Harngjou	PW:	Hangzhou
連 连	lián lian	V:	to connect, to join
水利	shuǐlì shoeilih	N:	irrigation
項 项	xiàng shianq	M:	measure word for achievement
成就	chéngjiù cherngjiow	N:	achievement, accomplishment

隋朝	Suícháo Sweichaur	N:	the Sui Dynasty (581-618)
中期	zhōngqī jongchi	TW:	middle period
交流	jiāoliú jiauliou	N:	exchange, interchange, communication
建設 建设	jiànshè jiannsheh	N: V:	construction to construct
鐵路 铁路	tiělù tieeluh	N:	railway
海	hǎi hae	N:	sea
地位	dìwèi dihwey	N:	position, status
不如	bùrú buru		not equal to, not as good as
無論 无论	wúlùn wuluenn	Adv:	no matter, regardless
貢獻 贡献	gòngxiàn gonqshiann	N: V:	contribution (of something with significance and abstract entity) to contribute

Sentence Patterns

1.　到底 ...（呢）？

An emphatic adverb used in a question -- "after all; really". The particle 嗎 can not be used with 到底.

⊙　長城到底有沒有防止北方的敵人呢？
Did the Great Wall protect the north from enemies after all?

(1)　A: 你到底懂了沒有？
A: Did you really understand?

B: 懂了。　　　（Don't use 到底 in a reply.）
B: I understood.

(2)　A: 你到底喜歡不喜歡這門課呢？
A: So, do you like this course or not?

B: 我不喜歡。
B: I don't like it.

2.　不如　　　not as good as

⊙　運河的地位就一天不如一天。
The importance of the Grand Canal decreases day by day.

(1)　看電影不如看書。
= 看書比看電影好。
Watching movies is not as good as reading books.
= Reading books is better than watching movies.

(2)　學物理不如學電子計算機。
Studying physics is not as good as studying computer science.

(3)　買美國車子不如買日本車，日本車又便宜又好。
Buying American cars is not as good as buying Japanese cars.
Japanese cars are both inexpensive and good.

A 不如 B SV   A is not as SV as B

(1) 妹妹不如姐姐漂亮。
The younger sister is not as pretty as the older one.

(2) 坐車不如走路方便。
Taking a car is not as convenient as walking.

(3) 我的英文不如你的英文好。
My English is not as good as yours.

一 M 不 如 一 M

(1) 經濟情況一年不如一年。
The economic situation is getting worse year after year.

(2) 他寫的小說一本不如一本。
The novels he writes get worse with every book.

3.   無 論 ... 都 / 也   no matter

⊙ 無論在國防上，經濟上，還是文化上，大運河對中國的
貢獻(都)比長城大得多。
No matter whether in terms of national defense, economics, or culture, the contribution of the Grand Canal to China is much greater than that of the Great Wall.

無 論 A 還 是 B

(1) 無論是冷的還是熱的我都不想喝。
No matter if it's cold or hot, I don't want to drink (anything).

(2) 無論你今天去還是明天去都行。
It doesn't matter whether you go today or tomorrow, both are alright.

無 論 A not A

(1)　　**無論貴不貴我都要買。**
Whether it's expensive or not, I want to buy it.

(2)　　**無論有錢沒錢，我都要去旅行。**
Whether I have money or not, I still want to travel.

無 論 with question words

(1)　　**在紐約，無論住在哪兒都很貴。**
In New York, no matter where you live it's very expensive.

(2)　　**我無論甚麼時候去找他，他都在家。**
Whenever I go to find him, he's always at home.

(3)　　**無論誰，都不認識這個人。**
No one recognizes this person.

(4)　　**無論多麼簡單的字他都寫不好。**
No matter how simple the character is, he still can't write it well.

(5)　　**無論花多少錢我都要買。**
Regardless of the amount of money that I have to spend, I will buy it.

Excercises

一．完成對話　(Complete the following dialogues with the expressions in parentheses.)

1.　A: 為什麼秦始皇在中國歷史上很有名？

　　B: ＿＿＿＿＿＿＿＿＿＿＿＿＿＿＿＿＿＿＿。
　　　　　　　　　　　　　　　　　　　　（影響）

2.　A: ＿＿＿＿＿＿＿＿＿＿＿＿＿＿＿＿＿＿＿？
　　　　　　　　　　　　　　　　　　　　（到底）

　　B: 他也許是昨天十點鐘給你打電話的。

3.　A: 為什麼美國建了一條從東到西的鐵路？

　　B: ＿＿＿＿＿＿＿＿＿＿＿＿＿＿＿＿＿＿＿。
　　　　　　　　　　　　　　　　　　　　（為了）

4.　A: 這個星期老師跟學生都得到學校來嗎？

　　B: ＿＿＿＿＿＿＿＿＿＿＿＿＿＿＿＿＿＿＿。
　　　　　　　　　　　　　　　　　　　　（無論）

5.　A: 美國的歷史長還是中國的歷史長？

　　B: ＿＿＿＿＿＿＿＿＿＿＿＿＿＿＿＿＿＿＿。
　　　　　　　　　　　　　　　　　　　　（比較）

二．改寫句子　(Rewrite the following sentences according to the words supplied below.)

1.　没有一個學過中文的人對中國歷史不熟悉。

　　B: ＿＿＿＿＿＿＿＿＿＿＿＿＿＿＿＿＿＿＿。
　　　　　　　　　　　　　　　　　　　　（只要）

2.　"美國的經濟情形越來越壞。"

　　＝＿＿＿＿＿＿＿＿＿＿＿＿＿＿＿＿＿＿＿。
　　　　　　　　　　　　　　　　　　　　（不如）

三． 翻譯 (Translation)

1. International transportation is getting more and more developed. Nowadays, people have more opportunities to travel in foreign countries.

2. Because of the affects of the Great Cultural Revolution, China's economic level is getting worse and worse.

3. Due to geographical restrictions, the area to the north of the Great Wall is not as developed as the area to the south.

4. In order to establish a good relationship with China, Nixon visited China's capital, Beijing. He also visited the Great Wall. In his view, the Great Wall is one of the greatest constructions in the world.

5. The Grand Canal connects the military (affairs) center in the north and the economic center in the south. The government relies on the canal to ship (raw) materials.

6. The Grand Canal connected the political and cultural centers of the north with the economic centers of the south in ancient China.

7. Although the population of this city is only 5% of that of the whole nation, it occupies an important place in politics, economy and national defense.

8. People who visit China will definitely go to visit the Great Wall. This construction was built by many many (thousands, ten thousands) Chinese people.

9. In his view, (the fact that) the area to the north of the river is much more backward than the area to the south (of it) has something to do with the development of transportation.

10. The contribution of the Grand Canal was much greater than the Great Wall in terms of national defense, economy and culture.

四． 作文 (Composition)

1. 要是你去過長城，請你說一說你的旅遊經驗。

2. 你是導遊員，你怎麼給去參觀長城的外國人介紹長城？

第十八課

胡 適

Vocabulary

胡適 胡适	Húshì Hwushyh		Hu Shih (1891-1962)
安徽	Ānhuī Anhuei	PW:	Anhwei Province
在地方上	zài dìfāngshàng tzay dih.fang.shanq	PW:	locally
去世	qùshì chiushyh	V:	to pass away, to die
能幹 能干	nénggàn nenggann	Adj:	capable
年輕 年轻	niánqīng nianching	Adj:	young
寡婦 寡妇	guǎfù goafuh	N:	widow
堅持 坚持	jiānchí jianchyr	V:	to insist on, to persist in
請 请	qǐng chiing	V:	to invite; to hire
要求	yāoqiú iau.chyou	N: V:	demands to demand
清早	qīngzǎo chingtzao	TW:	early in the morning
犯錯 犯错	fàncuò fanntsuoh	VO:	make a mistake
面前	miànqián miannchyan		in front of (a person), in the presence of

169

責備 责备	zébèi tzerbey	V:	to reproach, to scold
體罰 体罚	tǐfá tiifar	V:	to physically punish; corporal punishment
成名	chéngmíng cherngming	V:	to become famous
感激	gǎnjī gaanji	V:	to be grateful to, to thank
白話文 白话文	báihuàwén bairhuahwen	N:	vernacular language
文言文	wényánwén wenyanwen	N:	classical language
主張 主张	zhǔzhāng juujang	V: N:	to propose, to advocate proposal
文字	wénzì wentzyh	N:	the written language
反映	fǎnyìng faanyinq	V: N:	to reflect reflection
時代 时代	shídài shyrday	N:	era, period
文章	wénzhāng wenjang	N:	essay, article
留學 留学	liúxué lioushyue	VO:	to study abroad
西方	xīfāng shifang	Adj:	West(ern)
民主	mínzhǔ minjuu	N: Adj:	democracy democratic
恢復 恢复	huīfù hueifuh	V:	to restore, revive, recover
指出	zhǐchū jyychu	RV:	to point out
合理	hélǐ herlii	Adj:	"in accord with logic", reasonable, rational, logical

類 类	lèi ley	M/N:	a kind of
中	zhōng jong	Prep:	in ...
守節 守节	shǒujié shooujye	N: V:	maintenance of a widow's chastity (i.e. not remarrying) to maintain a widow's chastity
概念	gàiniàn gayniann	N:	general concept
婦女 妇女	fùnǚ fuhneu	N:	women
平等	píngděng pyngdeeng	Adj:	equal, fair
待遇	dàiyù dayyuh	N:	treatment
深刻	shēnkè shenkeh	Adj:	deep; profound, penetrating
批判	pīpàn pipann	N:	strong critcism; to criticize sharply
個人主義	gèrén zhǔyì gehren juuyih	N:	individualism
婦女解放	fùnǚ jiěfàng fuhneu jieefanq	N:	the emancipation of women
解放	jiěfàng jieefanq	V: N:	to emancipate, liberate emancipation, liberation
等	děng deeng		and so on; etc.
始終 始终	shǐzhōng shyyjong	Adv:	"beginning-end", from beginning to end, consistently
長期 长期	chángqī charngchi		for a long period of time
共產黨 共产党	Gòngchǎndǎng Gonqchaandaang	N:	"common property party", Communist Party
資本主義 资本主义	zīběnzhǔyì tzybeenjuuyih	N:	capitalism

171

資本 资本	zīběn tzybeen	N:	capital
資產階級	zīchǎnjiējí tzychaan jiejyi	N:	"capital class", bourgeoisie
階級 阶级	jiējí jiejyi	N:	(social) class
走狗	zǒugǒu tzoougoou	N:	"running dog", lackey (political term)
出賣 出卖	chūmài chumay	V:	to betray, to sell (someone) out
漢奸 汉奸	hànjiān hannjian	N:	Chinese traitor to China
政治宣傳 政治宣传	zhèngzhì xuānchuán jenqjyh shiuanchwan	N:	political propaganda
宣傳 宣传	xuānchuán shiuanchwan	V:	to publicize, to propagandize
巨大	jùdà jiuhdah	Adj:	enormous, large

Sentence Patterns

1. **V 甚 麼**　　　indefinite use meaning "not much" or "any"

⊙　雖然自己沒有受過甚麼教育，但是她堅持要胡適進最好的學校。
Although she herself had not received much education, she insisted that Hu Shih enter the best school.

(1)　我沒看過甚麼中文書。
I haven't read many Chinese books.

(2)　他沒甚麼錢，怎麼能買那麼貴的東西？
He doesn't have much money. How could he buy such expensive things?

(3)　明天下午我沒有甚麼事，你可以來。
Tomorrow afternoon I don't have much to do. You can come by.

(4)　他沒出過國所以沒受過甚麼西方教育的影響。
He hasn't been abroad, therefore he has not received much influence from Western education.

(5)　昨天我沒買甚麼東西所以錢沒用完。
I didn't buy much yesterday, so I haven't used up all the money..

2. **Question word V1, (就) Question word V2**

⊙　胡適主張怎麼說就怎麼寫。
Hu Shih advocated that you should write as you speak.

甚麼時代的人應該寫甚麼時代的文章。
One's writing should reflect the age in which he lives.

(1)　怎麼想就怎麼說。
Say whatever you think.

(2)　你怎麼寫我就怎麼寫。
I'll write however you write.

(3)　哪儿乾淨我就坐在哪儿。

173

I'll sit wherever it's clean.

(4)　　甚麼東西便宜就買甚麼。
Buy whatever is cheap.

(5)　　哪個好看要哪個。
(I) want whatever looks good.

(6)　　你吃甚麼我就吃甚麼。
I'll eat whatever you eat.

(7)　　誰有空誰去幫忙。
Whoever has time should help.

3. 才　　　　　conditional use

⊙　白話文是沒有學問的人才用的，受過教育的人都應該寫文言文。
Vernacular Chinese is only used by the uneducated. The educated should write in classical Chinese.

(1)　　屋子太黑了把電燈打開才看得清楚。
The room is too dark, you will only be able to see clearly if you turn on the light.

(2)　　寫完功課的人才可以回家。
Only those who have finished their homework may go home.

4. 是...而不是...

⊙　當時中國最需要的是民主和科學而不是恢復中國的舊制度，舊文化。
At that time, it was democracy and science that China needed most, not a revival of China's ancient system and old culture.

(1)   A: 你是中文專業還是物理專業？
A: Are you a Chinese or a physics major?

B: 我是中文專業而不是物理專業。
B: I am a Chinese major, not a physics major.

(2)   他是教授而不是學生。
He's a professor, not a student.

=   他不是學生而是教授。
He is not a student, but a professor.

Excercises

一．完成對話　　　(Complete the following dialogues with the expressions in parentheses.)

1.　A: 你在台北住了多久？你對台北這個城市熟不熟？

　　B: _____。
　　　　　　　　　　　　　　　　　　　　　　（才：only）

2.　A: 誰能在這個大學念書？

　　B: _____。
　　　　　　　　　　　　　　　　　　　（才：conditional）

3.　A: 他是你的朋友還是你的敵人？

　　B: _____。
　　　　　　　　　　　　　　　　　　（是 ... 而不是 ...）

　　A: 現在我知道了，原來他　_____。
　　　　　　　　　　　　　　　　　　（不是 ... 而是 ...）

4.　A: 你想住在哪個房間？

　　B: _____。
　　　　　　　　　　　　　　　　　　　　（question word）

二．改寫句子　　　(Rewrite the following sentences according to the words supplied below.)

1.　只要是你喜歡吃的東西，我就喜歡吃。

　　_____。
　　　　　　　　　　　　　　　　　　　（question word）

2.　要是你要看古代的文章你就得看得懂文言文。

　　_____。
　　　　　　　　　　　　　　　　　　　　　　（才）

三 ． 翻譯　　　(Translation)

1. Before Hu Shih promoted the vernacular language, Chinese wrote essays in the classical language. Except for educated people, nobody could read them.

2. Since he has lived outside of this country for many years, his concepts (way of thinking) have been influenced by the Western lifestyle.

3. What China needs most is to promote democracy and science, not to revive China's old system and culture.

4. At the end of the 19th century, many young people went abroad to study. They were influenced by the Western style of living. After they returned, they considered (thought) the old Chinese systems unreasonable.

5. Good parents do not reprimand their children in front of their children's friends.

6. Those people who disagreed with Hu Shih said that what China needed most was the restoration of traditional culture.

7. Women in America have severely criticized their unequal treatment.

8. You have made a great contribution to our country. We want to thank you. We will give you whatever you like.

四 ． 作文　　　(Composition)

1. 請你介紹一個美國歷史上有名的人。

2. 你覺得胡適提倡的觀念哪個對中國最要緊？為什麼？

第十九課

魯迅

Vocabulary

魯迅 鲁迅	Lǔ Xùn Luu Shiunn		Lu Hsun (1881-1936)
近代史	jìndàishǐ jinndayshyy	N:	early modern history
影響力 影响力	yǐngxiǎnglì yiingsheanglih	N:	power to influence
文學家 文学家	wénxuéjiā wenshyuejia	N:	man of letters, literatus
批評家 批评家	pīpíngjiā pipyngjia	N:	critic
出生	chūshēng chusheng	V:	to be born
浙江	Zhèjiāng Jehjiang	PW:	Chekiang Province
紹興 绍兴	Shàoxīng Shawshing	PW:	Shaoshing, a county of Chekiang
富裕	fùyù fuhyuh	Adj:	rich, prosperous (formal)
童年	tóngnián torngnian	N:	childhood (formal)
入獄 入狱	rùyù ruhyuh	VO:	to go to jail (literary)
突然	tūrán turan	Adv:	suddenly, unexpectedly
由	yóu you	Prep:	from
窮困 穷困	qióngkùn chyongkuenn	Adj:	impoverished (formal)

經歷	经历	jīnglì jinglih	N: V:	one's accumulated experiences to experience
體驗	体验	tǐyàn tiiyann	V: N:	to understand from first-hand experience first-hand experience
創作	创作	chuàngzuò chuanqtsuoh	N: V:	writings, work of art, literature to write, to create
回憶	回忆	huíyì hweiyih	N: V:	memories to recall
成了		chéngle cherng.le	V:	became
寫作	写作	xiězuò shieetzuoh	V: N:	to write (works of literature) writing
材料		cáiliào tsairliaw	N:	material (for a story, construction, etc.)
生病		shēng-bìng sheng-binq	VO:	to be sick
中醫	中医	zhōngyī jong'i	N:	doctor of Chinese medicine; Chinese medicine
不過	不过	búguò buguoh	Adj:	merely, only, just
有意		yǒuyì yeouyih	Adj:	intentional; to intend to
無意	无意	wúyì wuyih	Adj:	unintentional
騙子	骗子	piànzi pianntz	N:	a cheat, swindler
西醫	西医	xīyī shi'i	N:	Western medicine; doctor who practices Western medicine
治病		zhì-bìng jyh-binq	VO:	to treat a disease
偶然		ǒurán oouran	Adj: Adv:	by chance; unexpectedly unexpectedly
機會	机会	jīhuì ji'huey	N:	opportunity

精神	jīngshén jingshern	N:	spirit, energy
羣	qún chyun	M:	a group of, a herd of
愚昧	yúmèi yumey	Adj:	stupid, ignorant
消滅　消灭	xiāomiè shiaumieh	V:	to eradicate, obliterate
從事　从事	cóngshì tsorngshyh	V:	pursue (an occupation)
文藝　文艺	wényì wenyih	N:	the arts
喚醒　唤醒	huànxǐng huannshiing	RV:	to awaken (someone) (only abstract sense)
短篇	duǎnpiān doanpian	Adj:	short (of novels)
小説　小说	xiǎoshuō sheaushuo	N:	novel, story
狂人日記	Kuángrén rìjì Kwangren ryhjih		"Diary of a Madman", a short story by Lu Hsun (1918)
孔乙己	Kǒngyǐjǐ Koongyiijii		"Kong Yiji", name of a short story by Lu Hsun (1921 - 1922)
阿Ｑ正傳 阿Ｑ正传	A Q zhèngzhuàn A Q jenqjuann		"The True Story of Ah Q", a short story by Lu Hsun (1919)
藥　　药	Yào Yaw		"Medicine", a short story by Lu Hsun
著名	zhùmíng juhming	Adj:	famous (formal)
作品	zuòpǐn tzuohpiin	N:	a piece of artistic work
五四運動 五四运动	Wǔsì yùndòng Wuusyh yunndonq		May Fourth Movement (1919)
前後　前后	qiánhòu chyanhow		around, about (a certain time)

發表　发表	fābiǎo fabeau	V:	to publish, to express (an opinion) publicly
娛樂　娱乐	yúlè yuleh	N: V:	entertainment, amusement to entertain
知識分子 知识分子	zhīshìfènzǐ jyshyhfenntzyy	N:	an intellectual
認真　认真	rènzhēn rennjen	Adj:	conscientious, serious
重要	zhòngyào jonqyaw	Adj:	important
地位	dìwèi dihwey	N:	position, stand
古典	gǔdiǎn guudean	Adj:	classical
改良	gǎiliáng gaeliang	V:	to improve, to refine
嚴肅　严肃	yánsù yansuh	Adj:	serious, solemn
主角	zhǔjué juujyue	N:	main character, protagonist
受重視　受重视	shòu ... zhòngshì show ... jonqshyh	VO:	to be considered important by ..., to be valued by ...
重視　重视	zhòngshì jonqshyh	V:	to think highly, to consider as important
小人物	xiǎo rénwù sheau renwuh	N:	nobody, the little man
人物	rénwù renwuh	N:	characters (in a book), people, (political) figures
壓迫　压迫	yāpò iapoh	V: N:	to oppress oppression
貧困　贫困	pínkùn pynkuenn	Adj:	impoverished
農人　农人	nóngrén nongren	N:	peasants

181

失意	shīyì shy'yih	Adj:	dissapointed in one's life-time ambitions, frustrated
清末民初	Qīngmò Mínchū Chingmoh Minchu	TW:	at the end of the Ching dynasty and the beginning of the Republic of China
毫不	háobù haurbu		not at all
保留	bǎoliú baoliou	V:	to hold back, to not speak freely
揭露	jiēlù jieluh	V:	to expose
殘酷 残酷	cánkù tsarnkuh	Adj:	cruel
虛假 虚假	xūjiǎ shiujea	N: Adj:	falseness, hypocrisy false
中年	zhōngnián jongnian	N:	middle age
大量	dàliàng dahlianq	Adj:	a large quantity, a large number
雜文 杂文	záwén tzarwen	N:	an essay form made famous by Lu Hsun
無所不談 无所不谈	wúsuǒbùtán wusuoo.butarn		"nothing which is not discussed", willing to talk about anything and having opinions on many subjects
時事 时事	shíshì shyrshyh	N:	contemporary events
特點 特点	tèdiǎn tehdean	N:	"special points", characteristics
內容	nèiróng neyrong	N:	the content
帶 带	dài day	V:	to carry with (abstract), to bear, to have
諷刺 讽刺	fěngcì feengtsyh	Adj: V:	satiric to satirize

意味	yìwèi yihwey	N:	flavor (of piece of writing, speech, etc.), implications, nuances (formal)
廣大 广大	guǎngdà goangdah	Adj:	vast, wide
國事 国事	guóshì gwoshyh	N:	national affairs
時局 时局	shíjú shyrjyu	N:	the state (of the nation or world)
多方面	duō-fāngmiàn duo-fangmiann	Adj:	many aspects, multifaceted
關懷 关怀	guānhuái guanhwai	N: V:	concern to show concern for; to feel concern for
紀念 纪念	jìniàn jihniann	V: N:	to commemorate commemoration

Sentence Patterns

1. 由   from

⊙ 這種由富裕變到窮困的經歷讓魯迅體驗了不同的生活。
This type of experience, of becoming impoverished out of a prosperous background, made Lu Xun experience a different life first-hand.

     (1) 由古到今
From ancient times to today

2. 前後   around; about

⊙ (這些)著名的作品都是在五四運動前後發表的。
These famous works were all published around the May Fourth period.

     (1) 新年前後的飛機票特別難買。
Plane tickets around New Year's are particularly difficult to buy.

     (2) 文化大革命發生前後中國無論在各方面都很不安定。
Around the time of the Great Cultural Revolution, no matter in what aspect, China was very unstable.

3. 有的 ... 有的 ...   some ..., some ...

⊙ 有的是被壓迫的婦女，有的是貧困的農人，有的是失意的知識分子。
Some were oppressed women, some were impoverished farmers, some were disappointed intellectuals.

(1) 球場上有很多學生，有的打球，有的跑步。
There are a lot of students on the ball field, some are playing ball, some are running.

(2) 昨天我買的那些衣服，有的很便宜，有的很貴。
Of those clothes I bought yesterday, some were cheap, some were expensive.

(3) 他的朋友，有的是醫生，有的是作家。
Some of his friends are doctors, some are writers.

Excercises

一．完成對話　(Complete the following dialogues with the expressions in parentheses.)

1. A: 美國的人口多不多？

   B: _____。

   （之一）

2. A: 你喜歡不喜歡那篇小說？

   B: _____。

   （印象）

3. A: 魯迅怎麼改良社會？

   B: _____。

   （用...來...）

4. A: 假期的時候，學生做什麼？

   B: _____。

   （有的...有的...）

5. A: 我去中國旅行的時候應該去看哪些地方？

   B: _____。

   （值得）

二．改寫句子　(Rewrite the following sentences according to the words supplied below.)

1. 在我們家裡，没有一個人會用左手寫字。

   = _____。

   （連）

   = _____。

   （任何）

2. 放假的時候學生不是回家就是去旅行。

_____。

(有的...有的...)

三. 翻譯 (Translation)

1. He often publishes articles in newspapers. His articles reflect his viewpoint on the problems of Chinese society.

2. Although intellectuals showed their concerns regarding national affairs, their opinions were not considered important by the government.

3. Although your family's economic situation is not good, you still should let your child study abroad.

4. He was one of the most influential critics in modern literary history.

5. He is a doctor who practices Western medicine, however, when he gets sick, he sees a Chinese doctor to treat him. Therefore, I have a very bad impression of him.

四. 作文 (Composition)

請你說一說魯迅是一個怎麼樣的人。

第二十課

學生運動與文化大革命

Vocabulary

近代史	jìndàishǐ jinndayshyy	N:	modern history
叫人	jiàorén jiawren	V:	make (someone) ...
難忘　难忘	nánwàng nanwanq	Adj:	unforgettable (literary)
日子	rìzi ryhtz	N:	day (specific)
人民解放軍 人民解放军	rénmínjiěfàngjūn renminjieefanq jiun	N:	the Chinese People's Liberation Army
坦克車　坦克车	tǎnkèchē taankehche	N:	tank
機關槍　机关枪	jīguānqiāng jiguanchiang	N:	machine gun
天安門廣場 天安门广场	tiān'ānménguǎng chǎng tian'anmen goangchaang	PW:	Tian'anmen Square
廣場　广场	guǎngchǎng goangchaang	N:	public square
示威	shìwēi shyhuei	V: N:	"show force", demonstrate demonstration
羣衆　群众	qúnzhòng chyunjonq	N:	the masses
開槍　开枪	kāiqiāng kaichianq	VO:	to shoot
反革命	fǎngémìng faangerminq		counterrevolutionary

188

動亂	动乱	dòngluàn donqluann	N:	(political) turmoil; (social) upheaval
透過	透过	tòuguò towguoh		through
轉播	转播	zhuǎnbō joanbo	V:	relay (a radio or TV broadcast)
血腥		xiěxīng shieeshing	Adj:	bloody
鎮壓	镇压	zhènyā jeenia	V:	suppress (political)
憤怒	愤怒	fènnù fennnuh	Adj:	indignant
遊行	游行	yóuxíng youshyng	V: N:	demonstrate, parade, march demonstration, parade, march
采取	采取	cǎiqǔ tsaecheu	V:	to adopt (policy, method, etc.)
寬容	宽容	kuānróng kuanrong	Adj:	tolerant
加以		jiāyǐ jiayii		an empty verb which points attention to the verb following; to apply
壓制	压制	yāzhì iajyh	V: N:	to suppress suppression
甚至於	甚至于	shènzhìyú shennjyhyu	Conj:	even, so far as to, so much so that
懷疑	怀疑	huáiyí hwaiyi	N: V:	doubt, suspicion to suspect
繼續	继续	jìxù jihshiuh	V:	to continue
威脅	威胁	wēixié ueishye	V: N:	to threaten threat
安定		āndìng andinq	N: Adj:	stability stable
強硬		qiángyìng chyangyinq	Adj:	harsh, hard, rigid

189

手段	shǒuduàn shoouduann	N: tactics, method (usually dishonest)
逮捕	dàibǔ daybuu	V: to arrest
反政府	fǎnzhèngfǔ faanjenqfuu	Adj: anti-government
反	fǎn faan	V: to oppose
言論 言论	yánlùn yanluenn	N: expression of one's views
這才 这才	zhècái jehtsair	only now
平息	píngxī pyngshi	V: to cause to subside; to subside, to calm down
官方	guānfāng guanfang	Adj: official side
演變 演变	yǎnbiàn yeanbiann	V: to gradually develop
無 无	wú wu	V: without **無政府**: anarchy
相提并論 相提并论	xiāngtíbìnglùn shiangtyibinq luenn	mention A and B in the same breath
恰當 恰当	qiàdàng chiahdanq	Adj: suitable, appropriate
由	yóu you	Prep: by
發動 发动	fādòng fadonq	V: to initiate (political event)
目的	mùdì muhdih	N: purpose, goal
擁護 拥护	yōnghù ionghuh	N: to support (a leader)
少數 少数	shǎoshù shaoshuh	Adj: minority

當權 当权	dāngquán dangchyuan	Adj:	to be in power
領導 领导	lǐngdǎo liingdao	N:	leader, leadership
毛澤東 毛泽东	Máo Zédòng Mau Tzerdong		Mao Zedong
集權 集权	jíquán jyichyuan	N:	centralized authority
統治 统治	tǒngzhì toongjyh	V:	to rule, to reign
加上	jiāshàng jiashanq	V: Conj:	to add plus, and, in addition
內部	nèibù neybuh	Adj:	internal
權力 权力	quánlì chyuanlih	N:	authority, power
鬥爭 斗争	dòuzhēng dowjeng	N: V:	a struggle to struggle, to contend
盲目	mángmù mangmuh	Adj:	blind
崇拜	chóngbài chorngbay	N:	worship 個人崇拜: worship of a single person, ("personality cult")
混亂 混乱	hùnluàn huennluann	Adj: N:	chaotic chaos
恐怖	kǒngbù koongbuh	Adj:	terrifying
黑暗	hēi'àn hei'ann	Adj:	dark (as in the Dark Ages) (formal)
時期 时期	shíqī shyrchi	N:	a period of time
受到	shòudào showdaw	RV:	to suffer
迫害	pòhài pohhay	N: V:	persecution to persecute

到…的地步	dào ... de dìbù daw ... .de dihbuh		to reach a certain (undesirable) point
難以　难以	nányǐ nanyii		difficult to
令人	lìngrén linqren	V:	to make someone ...
地步	dìbù dihbuh	N:	stage, point
知名	zhīmíng jyming	Adj:	famous
被害	bèihài beyhay	V:	to be executed
在…之中	zài ... zhīzhōng tzay ... jyjong		within
關閉　关闭	guānbì guanbih	V:	to close, shut up
停止	tíngzhǐ tyngjyy	V:	to cease
毫無　毫无	háowú ... haurwu ...		not to have the slightest ...
價值　价值	jiàzhí jiahjyr	N:	value, worth
渡過　渡过	dùguò duhguoh	RV:	to live through, pass through
漫長　漫长	màncháng manncharng	Adj:	lengthy
寶貴　宝贵	bǎoguì baoguey	Adj:	precious
自覺　自觉	zìjué tzyhjyue	Adj:	self-conscious, having self-awareness, self-motivated, self-inspired
愛國　爱国	àiguó aygwo	V:	to be patriotic, to love one's country

行動　行动	xíngdòng shyngdonq	N:	action
持…的態度 持…的态度	chí … de tàidù chyr … .de tay.duh	VO:	to take an attitude of …
站在…的地位	zhàn zài … .de dìwèi jann tzay … .de dihwey	VO:	take a stand of …
對立　对立	duìlì dueylih	Adj:	to oppose, to be antagonistic to, to be antithetical to
而	ér erl	Conj:	but (literary)
然而	rán'ér ran'erl	Conj:	but, and yet (formal)
在…之下	zài … zhīxià tzay … jyshiah	Prep:	under
政治壓力	zhèngzhì yālì jenqjyh ialih	N:	political pressure
壓力　压力	yālì ialih	N:	pressure, stress
讀書人　读书人	dúshūrén dwushuren	N:	an intellectual, a scholar
屈服	qūfú chiufwu	V:	to surrender, yield
又一次	yòu yí-cì yow i-tsyh		once again
證明　证明	zhèngmíng jenqming	V: N:	to prove proof
放棄　放弃	fàngqì fanqchih	V:	to give up, abandon, renounce
粒	lì lih	M:	a grain of
種籽　种籽	zhǒngzǐ joongtzyy	N:	seed

若干	ruògān ruohgan	Adj: several N: a certain amount or number (formal)
發芽 发芽	fā-yá fa-ya	N: to germinate, sprout
茁壯 茁壮	zhuózhuàng jwojuanq	V: become strong
國民黨 国民党	Guómíndǎng Gwomindaang	N: Chinese Nationalist Party (KMT)
關切 关切	guānqiè guanchieh	N: deep concern

Sentence Patterns

1. 起 先 ... 後 來 ...   at first ... afterwards; in the beginning ... later

⊙ 中國政府起先採取了一種比較寬容的政策...後來政府就採取了比較強硬的手段。
The Chinese government at first adopted a rather generous policy ..., but then later the government adopted a relatively stronger stance.

(1) 起先沒有人發現這是一個問題，後來這個問題才引起了大家的注意。
At first no one discovered that this [matter] was a problem. Only later did this problem attract everyone's attention.

(2) 他起先在學校的餐廳洗碗，後來找到了秘書的工作。
At first he washed dishes in the school cafeteria, then later he found a secretarial job.

(3) 他起先不同意我的看法，後來倒覺得我的看法很有道理。
At first he disagreed with my opinion. Later, to my surprise, he felt that my perspective was very reasonable.

2. 加 以   literary expression which makes the verb more formal

⊙ 政府起先採取一種比較寬容的政策，並沒有立刻加以壓制。
The government at first adopted a rather tolerant policy, it did not in fact immediately apply suppression.

(1) 這個制度太落伍了，得加以改良才行。
This system is too old-fashioned; it must be improved.

(2) 請你對這件事的情形加以說明。
Please explain the (current) situation of this matter.

(3) 明天開會的時候我們會對這個問題加以討論。
At tomorrow's meeting, we will discuss this issue.

3. 甚至於　　　　　even to the degree that

⊙ 他們甚至於對共產黨和社會主義也表示了懷疑。
They even went so far as to be suspicious of the Communist Party and Socialism.

(1) 他沒出過國，甚至於沒去過紐約。
He hasn't been abroad. He hasn't even been to New York.

(2) 他甚麼人都不相信，甚至於連父親的話也不相信。
He doesn't believe anyone. It's to the point that he doesn't even believe what his own father says.

4. 由　　　introduces agent or doer of an action (written or formal use)

⊙ 文化大革命是由共產黨發動的。
The Cultural Revolution was initiated by the Communist Party.

(1) 這個計劃是由張先生寫的。
This plan was written by Mr. Chang.

(2) 我明天要到加州去所以這個星期屋子由你來整理。
Tomorrow I must go to California, so this week the house will be straightened up by you.

5. 加上　　　plus; furthermore

⊙ 因為毛澤東的集權統治加上共產黨內部的權力鬥爭....
Because of Mao Zedong's dictatorial rule plus the power struggles within the Communist Party.....

(1) 聰明加上努力使他成為一個偉大的科學家。
Brilliance in addition to diligence have made him a great scientist.

(2) 他做事非常小心，加上他很有能力，所以請他做這件事一定沒有問題。

196

He does things very carefully, plus he is very capable. Therefore if you ask him to do this thing there will certainly be no problem.

6. 到 ... 的 地 步   to the point where

⊙ 知識分子在這段期間所受到的迫害到了難以令人相信的地步。
The persecution that intellectuals received during this period reached a degree that was unbelievable.

(1) 中國的人口問題已經到了很嚴重的地步。
The population problem in China has already reached a very critical point.

(2) 他的病已經厲害到了沒法子治的地步。
His sickness has become so serious that it has reached the point where there is no cure.

(3) 他們的婚姻有問題，可是還沒有到離婚的地步。
There are problems in their marriage, but it hasn't reached the point of divorce.

7. 在 ... （之） 中   in the course of (written or formal use)

⊙ 在這十年之中，學校關閉了，生產停止了。
In the last ten years, the schools have closed down and production has stopped.

(1) 在學習中文的過程中我認識了許多中國文化。
In the course of studying Chinese I came to know (recognize) a great deal of Chinese culture.

(2) 老師在教課中也學到了許多新東西。
In the course of teaching the teacher also learned a great many new things.

8. 在 ... 之 下   under (a certain condition or situation)

197

⊙ 在政治壓力之下中國的讀書人卻從來沒有完全的屈服過。

Although under political pressure, China's educated class never completely surrendered.

(1) 在政治壓力之下，沒有人敢反對政府。

Under the political pressure, no one dared to oppose the government.

(2) 在老師的幫助之下，我的中文水平越來越高了。

With the help of my teacher, my Chinese proficiency level is gradually improving.

(3) 在社會保險制度之下，老年人的生活是有保障的。

Under the system of social security, the lives of the elderly are secured (protected).

9. 在 ... 上　　to lie in (abstract sense)

⊙ 中國的希望不在共產黨也不在國民黨而在教育，在知識分子對國事的關切上。

China's hope depends not on the Communist Party, nor the KMT, but on education and the intellectuals' concern with national affairs.

(1) 這個文學作品的價值在對社會的影響上。

The value of this literary work lies in its influence on society.

(2) 他對中國的貢獻不在文學而在思想的改良上。

His contribution to China was not in literature, but in the improvement of thought.

Excercises

一．完成對話　(Complete the following dialogues with the expressions in parentheses.)

1．A: 他會不會說中文？

B: ＿＿＿＿＿＿＿＿＿＿＿＿＿＿＿＿＿＿＿。
　　　　　　　　　　　　　　　　（甚至於）

2．A: 紐約的交通怎麼樣？

B: ＿＿＿＿＿＿＿＿＿＿＿＿＿＿＿＿＿＿＿。
　　　　　　　　　　　　　（到了...的地步）

3．A: 這個城市的生活水平高不高？

B: ＿＿＿＿＿＿＿＿＿＿＿＿＿＿＿＿＿＿＿。
　　　　　　　　　　　　　（起先...後來）

二．改寫句子　(Rewrite the following sentences according to the words supplied below.)

1．他為了學英文到美國來留學。

= ＿＿＿＿＿＿＿＿＿＿＿＿＿＿＿＿＿＿＿。
　　　　　　　　　　　　　　　　（目的）

2．中國政府說胡適是帝國主義的走狗。

= ＿＿＿＿＿＿＿＿＿＿＿＿＿＿＿＿＿＿＿。
　　　　　　　　　　　　　　　　（比成）

3．因為受到政府的壓迫，已經生了個孩子的人只好墮胎。

= ＿＿＿＿＿＿＿＿＿＿＿＿＿＿＿＿＿＿＿。
　　　　　　　　　　　　　　（在...之下）

4．他批評我以前我根本不知道自己有這個缺點。

= ＿＿＿＿＿＿＿＿＿＿＿＿＿＿＿＿＿＿＿。
　　　　　　　　　　　　　　　　（這才）

三．翻譯　　　(Translation)

1. At the end of 1986, many Chinese college students adopted the approach of (staging) demonstrations to demand democracy and freedom from the government.

2. This was the first student movement to occur in China since the Chinese Communist Party took over (obtain) political power in 1949.

3. However, the Chinese government was willing to give them (open) freedom of speech only within a certain scope.

4. After the government arrested many of the students who joined the movement, the movement subsided.

四．　作文　　(Composition)

請你談一談你所知道的中國或者美國的學生運動。

第二十一課

外國地名的中文翻譯

Vocabulary

地名		dìmíng dihming	N:	place name
分不開	分不开	fēnbukāi fenbukai	RV:	cannot be separated
必須	必须	bìxū bihshiu	Aux:	must; have to
相關	相关	xiāngguān shiangguan	Adj:	related
了解		liǎojiě leaujiee	V:	to understand
過去	过去	guòqù guohchiuh	N:	past
環境	环境	huánjìng hwanjinq	N:	environment
空間	空间	kōngjiān kongjian	N:	space
必要		bìyào bihyaw	Adj:	necessary
知識	知识	zhīshi jyshyh	N:	knowledge
採用	采用	cǎiyòng tsaeyonq	V:	to adopt; to employ
音譯	音译	yīnyì inyih	N:	"sound translation"; transliteration
意譯	意译	yìyì yihyih	N:	"meaning translation"; translation
並用	并用	bìngyòng binqyonq	V:	to use concurrently

201

原則　原则	yuánzé yuantzer	N:	principle
聲音　声音	shēngyīn sheng'in	N:	sound; voice
相似	xiāngsì shiangsyh	Adj:	similar
非洲	Fēizhōu Feijou	PW:	Africa
成立	chénglì chernglih	V:	to establish
至今	zhìjīn jyhjin		up to now (written)
譯名　译名	yìmíng yihming	N:	translated name
如	rú ru	V:	for example; such as
尼日利亞	Nírìlìyà Niryhlihyah	PW:	Nigeria
坦桑尼亞	Tǎnsāngníyà Taansangniyah	PW:	Tanzania
阿爾及利亞	Ā'ěrjílìyà Ah'eeljyilihyah	PW:	Algeria
等	děng deeng		and so on
國　　国	guó gwo	N:	country
固定	gùdìng guhdinq	Adj:	fixed, solidified, entrenched
更改	gēnggǎi genggae	V:	change
國名　國名	guómíng gwoming	N:	name of a country
簡化　简化	jiǎnhuà jeanhuah	V:	to simplify

中文化	Zhōngwénhuà Jongwenhuah	V: to Sinicize
表面	biǎomiàn beaumiann	N: surface
痕跡	hénjī hernji	N: trace; vestige
亞美利亞	Yàměilìjiā Yahmeeilihjia	PW: America
俄國　俄国	èguó ehgwo	PW: the U.S.S.R., Soviet Union
蘇維埃　苏维埃	Sūwéi'āi Suwei'ai	PW: The Soviet Union
不列顛　不列颠	Búlièdiān Buliehdian	PW: Great Britain
法國　法国	fà (fǎ) guó fah (faa) gwo	PW: France
法蘭西　法兰西	Fǎlánxī Faalanshi	PW: France
德國　德国	Déguó Dergwo	PW: Germany
德意志	Déyìzhì Deryihjyh	PW: Germany
奧國　奥国	Àoguó Awgwo	PW: Austria
奧地利	Àodìlì Awdihlih	PW: Austria
以上	yǐshàng yiishanq	the above
美洲	Měizhōu Meeijou	PW: American continent
洲	zhōu jou	N: continent
及	jí jyi	Conj: and (literary)

亞洲　亚洲	Yàzhōu Yahjou	PW: Asia
亞細亞　亚细亚	Yàxìyà Yahshihyah	PW: Asia
歐羅巴　欧罗巴	Ouluóbā Ouluoba	PW: Europe
北美	Běiměi Beeimeei	PW: North America
加拿大	Jiā'nádà Jia'nadah	PW: Canada
中美	Zhōngměi Jongmeei	PW: Central America
墨西哥	Mòxīgē Mohshige	PW: Mexico
南美	Nánměi Nanmeei	PW: South America
巴西	Bāxī Bashi	PW: Brazil
智利	Zhìlì Jyhlih	PW: Chili
阿根廷	Āgēntíng Ahgentyng	PW: Argentina
菲律賓　菲律宾	Fēilǜbīn Feiluhbin	PW: The Phillipines
新加坡	Xīnjiāpō Shinjiapo	PW: Singapore
印度尼西亞	Yìndùnníxīyà Yinnduhnishiyah	PW: Indonesia
印尼	Yìnní Yinn'ni	PW: Indonesia
葡萄牙	Pútáoyá Pwutaurya	PW: Portugal
西班牙	Xībānyá Shibanya	PW: Spain

義大利 意大利	Yìdàlì Yihdalih	PW:	Italy
波蘭 波兰	Bōlán Bolan	PW:	Poland
人類 人类	rénlèi renley	N:	mankind
文明古國	wénmínggǔguó wenmingguu gwo	N:	a country with an ancient civilization 文明: civilization 古: ancient 國: country
希臘 希腊	Xīlà Shilah	PW:	Greece (Hellas)
埃及	Āijí Aijyi	PW:	Egypt
稱爲 称为	chēngwéi chengwei	V:	to be called; to be named
某	mǒu moou		a certain ...
直接	zhíjiē jyrjie	Adv:	directly
南端	nánduān nanduan		the southern end
好望角	Hǎowàngjiǎo Haowangjeau	PW:	Cape of Good Hope
象牙海岸	Xiàngyáhǎi'àn Shianqya'hae'ann	PW:	The Ivory Coast
牛津	Niújīn Nioujin	PW:	Oxford
黃石公園	Huángshí gōngyuán Hwangshyr gongyuan	PW:	Yellowstone National Park
猶他 犹他	Yóutā Youta	PW:	Utah

省會 省会	shěnghuì sheenghuey	N:	provincial or state capital
鹽湖城　盐湖城	Yánhúchéng Yanhwucherng	PW:	Salt Lake City
耶魯大學	Yēlǔdàxué Ieluudahshyue	N:	Yale University
新港	Xīn'gǎng Shin'gaang	PW:	New Haven
長島 长岛	Chángdǎo Charngdao	PW:	Long Island
靠近	kàojìn kawjinn	Adj:	near; close to
北極 北极	Běijí Beeijyi	PW:	The North Pole
冰島 冰岛	Bīngdǎo Bingdao	PW:	Iceland
洋	yáng yang	N:	ocean
印度洋	Yìndùyáng Yinnduhyang	PW:	Indian Ocean
太平洋	Tàipíngyáng Taypyngyang	PW:	Pacific Ocean
大西洋	Dàxīyáng Dahshiyang	PW:	Atlantic Ocean
北冰洋	Běibīngyáng Beeibingyang	PW:	Arctic Ocean
南冰洋	Nánbīngyáng Nanbingyang	PW:	Antarctic Ocean
地中海	Dìzhōnghǎi Dihjonghae	PW:	Meditteranean Sea
紅海	Hónghǎi Hornghae	PW:	Red Sea
黑海	Hēihǎi Heihae	PW:	Black Sea

特性	tèxìng tehshinq	N:	characteristics
南非共和國	Nánfēi gònghéguó Nanfei gonqhergwo	PW:	The Republic of South Africa
南斯拉夫	Nánsīlāfū Nansylhafu	PW:	Yugoslavia
外蒙古	Wàiménggǔ Waymengguu	PW:	Outer Mongolia
印度	Yìndù Yinnduh	PW:	India
新德里	Xīndélǐ Shinderlii	PW:	New Delhi
羅德島　罗德岛	Luódédǎo Luoderdao	PW:	Rhode Island
新澤西　新泽西	Xīnzéxī Shintzershi	PW:	New Jersey
新奧爾良	Xīn'àoěrliáng Shin'aweel'liang	PW:	New Orleans
劍橋　剑桥	Jiànqiáo Jiannchyau	PW:	Cambridge
好些	hǎoxiē haoshie		quite a lot
由	yóu you		from
高麗　高丽	Gāolì Gaulih	PW:	former name for Korea
琉球	Liúqiú Liouchyou	PW:	Ryukyou (Okinawa)
忘記　忘记	wàngjì wanqjih	V:	to forget
越南	Yuènán Yuehnan	PW:	Vietnam

重要	zhòngyào jonqyaw	Adj:	important
都市	dūshì dushyh	N:	metropolis
港口	gǎngkǒu gaangkoou	N:	port; harbor
華盛頓 华盛顿	Huáshèngdùn Hwashenqduenn	PW:	Washington, D.C.
莫斯科	Mòsīkē Mohsyke	PW:	Moscow
倫敦 伦敦	Lúndūn Luenduen	PW:	London
巴黎	Bālí Bali	PW:	Paris
東京 东京	Dōngjīng Dongjing	PW:	Tokyo

Sentence Patterns

1. 使   to make; to allow

⊙ 歷史使我們了解那個國家的過去；地理使我們認識那個國家的環境。
History allows us to understand that nation's past; geography makes us aware of that nation's environment.

     (1) 三年的工作經驗使他變成一個獨立的人。
Three years of independent work have made him become an independent individual.

     (2) 這件事使我們注意到社會上的問題。
This event made us take notice of the problems of society.

2. 只要   as long as

⊙ 音譯的外國地名只要是聲音相似的字就可以了。
When translating the names of foreign countries by sound, as long as the words selected sound similar to the original, then it's fine.

     (1) 只要是學過中文的人就看得懂這本書。
As long as you have learned Chinese, then you can understand this book.

     (2) 你不必來，只要給我打個電話就行了。
You don't need to come. As long as you give me a call it's alright.

3. 如 = 像   such as

⊙ 如美國，俄國...等。
... such as America, the Soviet Union, etc.

     (1) 我去過的地方很多：如紐約，倫敦，台北。
I've been to many places, such as New York, London, Taipei.

(2) 這個學校的系都很好，如物理系，化學系都是美
國最有名的。
This school's departments are all very good, for instance the physics department and the chemistry department are both the most famous in the US.

4. 以上　　　the above

⊙ 以上這些國家...
the above countries ...

(1) 以上我所說的話你們都懂了嗎？
Do you understand what I've said up to now (so far)?

(2) 以上這些題目都是跟歷史有關係的。
The above topics are related to history.

...以上

(1) 三十塊錢以上的東西我不願意買。
I'm not willing to buy anything that costs more than 30 dollars.

(2) 二十一歲以上的人才可以喝酒。
Only those people 21 years old and above may drink.

5. 除了...（以外），（其他）都...
except for ... , other(s) ...

⊙ 除了美國在美洲，...其他國家都在歐洲。
Except for the US in North America, ... the other countries are all located in Europe.

(1) 除了我以外其他的學生都對這門課沒有興趣。
Except for me, all the other students aren't interested in this class.

(2) 除了唱歌以外他甚麼都不會。
Except for singing, there's nothing else he can do.

(3) 除了這本書，別的我都看過了。
I have read all the other books except this one.

6. （由）...翻譯成...   to translate from ... to ...

⊙   亞洲的好些國名是由中文翻譯成英文的。
A number of Asian countries' names were translated from Chinese into English.

    (1)   這本小說是由法文翻譯成中文的。
This novel has been translated from French into Chinese.

    (2)   我想把他寫的詩翻譯成中文。
I want to translate his poems into Chinese.

Excercises

一．完成對話　　(Complete the following dialogues with the expressions in parentheses.)

1.　A: 哪些都市是重要的港口？

　　B: ＿＿＿＿＿＿＿＿＿＿＿＿＿＿＿＿＿＿＿＿＿＿＿。
　　　　　　　　　　　　　　　　　　　　　（像）

2.　A: 這本書的價錢貴不貴？

　　B: ＿＿＿＿＿＿＿＿＿＿＿＿＿＿＿＿＿＿＿＿＿＿＿。
　　　　　　　　　　　　　　　　　　　　　（以上）

3.　A: 中國的人口問題解決了沒有？

　　B: ＿＿＿＿＿＿＿＿＿＿＿＿＿＿＿＿＿＿＿＿＿＿＿。
　　　　　　　　　　　　　　　　　　　　　（至今）

4.　A: 你的中文進步了沒有？

　　B: ＿＿＿＿＿＿＿＿＿＿＿＿＿＿＿＿＿＿＿＿＿＿＿。
　　　　　　　　　　　　　　　　　　　　（一天比一天）

二．用口語解釋下面的詞　　(Explain the following terms in vernacular Chinese)

　　　以及，及，由，如，至今，稱為

1.　紐約是美國的經濟及政治中心。
2.　這個名字是由英文翻譯成中文的。
3.　如越南、韓國、日本等這幾個國家都在亞洲。
4.　我至今還不知道他住在哪儿。
5.　有些人把中國人稱為唐人。

三. 　　翻譯練習 　(Translation Exercise)

請你查出下面這些英文地名的中文翻譯然後說明這些地名翻譯
的原則是甚麼。

1. West Point
2. Waterloo
3. Hawaii
4. New Mexico
5. San Francisco

第二十二課

中 東 戰 爭

Vocabulary

中東 中东	zhōngdōng jongdong	PW:	Middle East
戰爭 战争	zhànzhēng jannjeng	N:	war
總統 总统	zǒngtǒng tzoongtoong	N:	president (for a nation)
布什	Bùshí Buhshyr		Bush, proper name
東部 东部	dōngbù dongbuh	PW:	"East Part", east
下令	xià-lìng shiah-linq	VO:	to order, to give an order (by officials)
轟炸 轰炸	hōngzhà hongjah	V:	to bomb
伊拉克	Yīlākè ilhakeh	PW:	Iraq
出兵	chū-bīng chu-bing	VO:	to dispatch troops
打	dǎ daa	V:	to attack, hit; to fight a battle
佔領 占领	zhànlǐng jannliing	V:	to occupy (land)
科威特	Kēwēitè keueiteh	PW:	Kuwait
公理	gōnglǐ gonglii	N:	justice
場 场	chǎng chaang	M:	AN for battle

214

打仗	dǎzhàng daajanq	VO: to fight a battle; to wage a war
石油	shíyōu shyryou	N: oil, petroleum
利益	lìyì lihyih	N: benefit, profit
强	qiáng chyang	Adj: strong, powerful
應該　应该	yīnggāi inggai	Aux.: should, ought to
阻止	zǔzhǐ tzuujyy	V: to prevent, to stop
巴拿馬　巴拿马	Bānámǎ Banamaa	PW: Panama
屠殺　屠杀	túshā twusha	V: to massacre, to slaughter
立陶宛	Lìtáowǎn Lihtaurwoan	PW: Lithuania
公平	gōngpíng gongpyng	Adj: fair, just
所謂　所谓	suǒwèi suoowey	Adj: so-called
具體　具体	jùtǐ jiuhtii	Adj: concrete, specific
指揮　指挥	zhǐhuī jyyhuei	V: to command, to direct, to conduct N: command, order
支持	zhīchí jychyr	V: to support N: support
愛國　爱国	àigúo aygwo	VO: to love one's country Adj: patriotic
愚蠢	yúchǔn yuchoen	Adj: stupid, foolish
殖民地	zhímíndì jyrmindih	N: colony

過去 过去	guòqù guohchiuh	V:	to pass
遠見 远见	yuǎnjiàn yeuanjiann	N:	foresight
管	guǎn goan	V:	to mind, to manage, to take care of, to administer
國內 国内	guónèi gwoney	Adj: PW:	domestic within the country
安定	āndìng andinq	Adj:	stable, settled (of situations or circumstances)
帶來 带来	dàilái daylai	VC:	to bring along

Sentence Patterns

1. 為了...才

⊙ 美國是為了維持世界公理才打這場仗的。
Only to maintain world justice did the U.S. fight this war.

(1) 他是為了學習中文才到中國去的。
He went to China for the purpose of studying Chinese.

(2) 你是不是為了畢業以後能找到一份好工作才學習物理的？
Did you study physics in order to find a good job after graduation?

(3) 為了孩子能受到很好的照顧，母親才決定待在家裡。
It was only for the reason that the children could be well taken care of that the mother decided to stay at home.

是為了 Noun

(1) 你跟他結婚是不是為了錢？
是不是為了錢你才跟他結婚？
= Did you marry him just for his money?

(2) 我這麼作是為了自己的將來。
= 為了自己的將來我才這麼作。
I did it this way out of consideration for my own future.

Excercises

一．完成對話　　(Complete the following dialogues with the expressions in parentheses.)

1.　A: 你去年為甚麼上中國去了？

　　B: _____。
　　　　　　　　　　　　　　　　（為了...才...）

2.　A: 美國為甚麼出兵到東去？

　　B: _____。
　　　　　　　　　　　　　　　　（...是為了...）

3.　A: 在我看來，同居跟結婚沒有甚麼不同。

　　B: 我不以為然，_____。
　　　　　　　　　　　　　　　　（相提並論）

4.　A: 為甚麼六四以後中國人不敢回中國去？

　　B: _____。
　　　　　　　　　　　　　　　　（威脅）

二．翻譯　　(Translation)

1.　War cannot solve all the problems in the world. It will only bring with it more and more problems.

2.　I don't support the way that the government establishes a new world order by means of violence.

3.　The Vietnam War and the Persian Gulf War are two different things. It is unfair to draw a parallel between these two wars.

4.　When China fought with Japan, Japan sent many airplanes to bomb Nanking. Thousands of people were massacred.

5　The government controls the television. Therefore, news broadcasts are filled with government propaganda.

6. We must stop the invasion of one country by another country. In this aspect, economic sanctions might be effective.

三．作文　　(Composition)

1. 你認為美國應該不應該出兵到中東去？為甚麼？
2. 談愛國。